Edit

As I was writing the editor's note this year, several surprising things happened. Congestion pricing—hotly debated for at least twenty years—was delayed, possibly forever, just days before implementation. Hot dog–eating world record holder Joey Chestnut (at seventy-six dogs, with buns) was dropped from Nathan's Famous Fourth of July Hot Dog Eating Contest for, of all things, endorsing a company that makes *meatless* hot dogs. The *Times* reported on an old-style Brooklyn red-sauce joint—Sam's in Cobble Hill—that stays in business not by making pizza, but by playing a version of itself on film. And James Kane, a pandemic-minted magnet fisherman, pulled a safe filled with about $70,000 in black sludge-coated $100 bills from a creek in Flushing Meadows Corona Park. As Nancy Franklin put it in the *New Yorker*, "It's a city you never get tired of; it's a city that tires you out. You're crazy about it; it drives you crazy. There's no getting around it: New York makes no sense." Or as gossip columnist Cindy Adams might say, "Only in New York, kids, only in New York."

This year's almanac is chock-full of more "only in New York" moments of the current—performances, art exhibitions, and film festivals—and the vintage kind. And hopefully a few surprises, too. Please check with the venues before you head out, as dates are subject to change, and be on the lookout for newly announced events to fill in as they arrive. Let's hope they make you crazy about the city, not the other way around.

THE FIVE-BOROUGH FASHION FORECAST: As New York City gets down to business in 2025, the inevitable return to the office will demand a new approach to workwear. Sartorial professionalism will be back in a big way, but it will be a far cry from the suited and booted uniforms of corporate power players from days gone by. Instead, expect creative twists on tailored pieces and pops of personality to jazz up any job.

After several seasons of voluminous sleeves, skirts, and outerwear, we can expect silhouettes to decrease dramatically as a more streamlined sensibility emerges. Color, too, will quiet down—with muted tones and no-nonsense neutrals coming to the fore. Luxury will continue to be downplayed, with subtle indicators of status replacing ostentatious displays of wealth. Logomania is all but dead, which spells trouble for Fifth Avenue and Canal Street alike. But innovative design will prevail among burgeoning fashion creators, with an emphasis on reimagining classics and developing textile technology. The growing prevalence of artificial intelligence might very well drive tech-weary consumers toward products that bring them closer to the natural world—think botanical design motifs, eco-friendly dyes, and fabrics sans synthetic materials.

The cultural chasm that divides Generations X, Y, and Z points to the likelihood of divergent style trajectories according to age group. The reclamation of "girlhood" among younger women could see the popular coquette aesthetic develop into similarly playful trends rooted in youthfulness. Gen Z's continued obsession with Y2K teen styles might amuse those who wore them the first time around, who are instead gravitating toward styles that indicate maturity—in the form of bodycon dresses that celebrate womanly figures, or pieces associated with distinctively dressed members of the fashion gerontocracy. We've already seen the breezy cardigans of the Coastal Grandma and the natty vests of the Eclectic Grandpa—could our elders be the next influencers? Or could the growing discontent with the fast fashion cycle put a damper on the dizzying merry-go-round of microtrends? Wherever they seek their style inspiration, you can be sure that the urban dwellers across the five boroughs will continue to give New York its uniquely diverse fashion flair.

JANUARY

FOR SOME (MOSTLY OUT-OF-TOWNERS), the idea of New Year's Eve in New York City conjures up images of velvet ropes, sequins, high heels, and exorbitant prix fixe menus. For the highbrow glitterati, it's the black-tie Metropolitan Opera Gala. But for 4,800 heroic New Yorkers, the holiday means one thing: a frigid **four-mile dash through Central Park with the New York Road Runners** as the clock strikes midnight. January's icy doldrums are usually the last chance to catch all of those "must-see" **fall exhibitions** that you didn't get around to, from the highbrow—*Sèvres Extraordinaire! Sculpture from 1740 until Today* at Bard Graduate Center or *The African Origin of Civilization* at the Metropolitan Museum of Art—to the quirky—*Liberty the Tattooed Lady: The Great Bartholdi Statue as Depicted in Tattooing* at Williamsburg's City Reliquary Museum. **Joshua Bell is coming to the New York Philharmonic,** and the **Exponential Festival** presents experimental theater around Brooklyn all month.

PROFESSOR VATICINATE SAYS, *the year begins wet every which way. By January's second week, ill winds blow rain and wet snow. Hopefully a "wintermission" for Inauguration Day, then slushes and sloshes will require galoshes. As we all know, slushy roads can be a wet slide story. The month comes to an end bleak and bleary, slushy and dreary. In fact, some believe that a snow removal budget is really a slush fund.*

NORMALS FOR
CENTRAL PARK

Avg. high: 39.5°
Avg. low: 27.9°
Avg. rainfall: 3.64"
Avg. snowfall: 8.8"

By far and away, the coldest stretch of weather in NYC history occurred from December 29, 1917, through January 1, 1918. On each of those four days, the low temperature registered below zero: −6°, −13°, −7°, and −4°. And during the Times Square ball drop, the temperature fell to a frigid +1° with a north wind at 9 mph, making for a bitter cold wind chill temperature of −18°.

January is the cloudiest month: 14 days average more than 8/10 cloud cover.

SKY WATCH: During January, we will see Mars at its brightest and closest to Earth. On the 12th, it will be 59.7 million miles away. This month it will be visible all night long, appearing like a bright yellow-orange star. Between 9:19 p.m. and 10:35 p.m. on the 13th, the full Moon will pass directly in front of Mars, and the "Twin Stars," Castor and Pollux, will point directly toward Mars on the 16th.

ANNALS OF THE NIGHT SKY

If you have ever been to Grand Central Terminal, you have no doubt noticed the stylized map of the night sky depicted on its lofty ceiling. The constellations that are portrayed are those of our current winter sky and were copied directly from the renowned 1603 star atlas *Uranometria*. The brightest stars are marked by light bulbs, creating an eye-catching effect. One faux pas, dating back to when the star map was rendered in 1913, is that, with the exception of Orion, the stars are arranged in reverse order.

NYC BOOK OF THE MONTH
Sister Carrie by Theodore Dreiser (1900)

The tumult of an urbanizing, modernizing nation is personified in Carrie, a midwestern country girl who trades her small-town morals for material wealth in Chicago and later New York. Left in her wake is her discarded lover, Hurstwood, who tumbles from middle-class comfort to being a scab in the violent real-life Brooklyn Trolley Strike that started in January 1895.

NYC MOVIE OF THE MONTH
Shaft, directed by Gordon Parks, starring Richard Roundtree, Moses Gunn, and Charles Cioffi (1971)

Shaft has a plot as goofy as it is New York-y—a Black detective saving the daughter of a hustler who has been kidnapped by the mafia. But Roundtree's embodiment of the first Black action hero was irresistible—and started the "blaxploitation" genre. The opening scene captures a real-life Gay Activists Alliance protest march on West 42nd Street.

January has 31 days.

● Dec. 30–Jan. 5

"No other city is so spitefully
incoherent."
—James Baldwin

30 MONDAY

☀ 7:21 AM / 4:38 PM   ● NEW MOON

Radio City Rockettes Christmas
Spectacular (through Jan. 5)

31 TUESDAY

☀ 7:21 AM / 4:39 PM

New Year's Eve

New York Road Runners Midnight
Run in Central Park

WEDNESDAY

☀ 7:20 AM / 4:39 PM

New Year's Day • *Kwanzaa ends.*

Coney Island Polar Bear Plunge

2 THURSDAY

☼ 7:20 AM / 4:40 PM

Hanukkah ends.

Metropolitan Opera presents
The Magic Flute—Holiday Presentation.

3 FRIDAY

☼ 7:20 AM / 4:41 PM

New York Philharmonic
presents Richard Strauss's
Also sprach Zarathustra (Jan. 2–7).

4 SATURDAY

☼ 7:20 AM / 4:42 PM

Three Kings Day celebration at
The Clemente, co-organized with
Teatro SEA

5 SUNDAY

☼ 7:20 AM / 4:43 PM

NYCRUNS Frozen Penguin 5K
in Central Park

Jan. 6–12

"That is the city paradox . . . you have to go right into the center of things, immerse in the crowds, and there you find the very tools that allow you to vanish."
—Thomas Beller

6 MONDAY

☼ 7:20 AM / 4:44 PM ◐ 1ST QUARTER

Epiphany/Three Kings Day

Celebrate Three Kings Day at El Museo del Barrio.

7 TUESDAY

☼ 7:20 AM / 4:45 PM

Orthodox Christmas Day

Metropolitan Opera presents a new production of *Aida* (Dec. 31–May 9).

8 WEDNESDAY

☼ 7:19 AM / 4:46 PM

Joshua Bell plays Dvořák and Tchaikovsky at the New York Philharmonic (through Jan. 11).

9 THURSDAY

☼ 7:19 AM / 4:47 PM

Metropolitan Opera presents *Tosca* (through Jan. 23).

10 FRIDAY

☼ 7:19 AM / 4:48 PM

Jazz at Lincoln Center presents Unity Jazz Festival (and 11th)

11 SATURDAY

☼ 7:19 AM / 4:49 PM

Last chance to see *Life Dances On: Robert Frank in Dialogue* at MoMA

12 SUNDAY

☼ 7:18 AM / 4:50 PM

Last chance to see *Liberty the Tattooed Lady: The Great Bartholdi Statue as Depicted in Tattooing* at the City Reliquary Museum

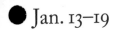 Jan. 13–19

"New York . . . would seem on the face of it to be founded on progress, on change, on the bulldozing of what has failed to make way for the next thing, the thing after that, the future."
—Lucy Sante

13 MONDAY

☾ 7:18 AM / 4:51 PM ○ FULL MOON

Met Orchestra Chamber Ensemble at Weill Recital Hall, Carnegie Hall

14 TUESDAY

☼ 7:18 AM / 4:52 PM

Orthodox New Year

BAM Next Wave presents *Voices* by Margarita Athanasiou, part of ONX Studio's *TECHNE* (and Jan. 12, 15).

15 WEDNESDAY

☼ 7:17 AM / 4:53 PM

Metropolitan Opera presents *La Bohème* (through Jun. 6).

16 THURSDAY

☼ 7:17 AM / 4:54 PM

Jazz at Lincoln Center presents Cool School and Hard Bop: The JLCO with Wynton Marsalis (through Jan. 18).

17 FRIDAY

☼ 7:16 AM / 4:56 PM

BAM Next Wave presents *Secret Garden* by Stephanie Dinkins, part of ONX Studio's *TECHNE* (and Jan. 16, 18–19).

18 SATURDAY

☼ 7:16 AM / 4:57 PM

Final opportunity to see *Thomas Schütte* at MoMA

19 SUNDAY

☼ 7:15 AM / 4:58 PM ♒ AQUARIUS

Last chance to catch *The Way I See It: Selections from the KAWS Collection* at the Drawing Center

Jan. 20–26

"The gonglike, tornadolike, oceanic, unceasing roar and tumult of this bustling street makes it less inviting than it otherwise would be."
—Joel H. Ross, 1851

20 MONDAY

☼ 7:15 AM / 4:59 PM

Martin Luther King Jr. Day

21 TUESDAY

☼ 7:14 AM / 5:00 PM   ☽ 3RD QUARTER

Chicago Symphony Orchestra plays Carnegie Hall.

22 WEDNESDAY

☼ 7:13 AM / 5:01 PM

Carnegie Hall presents Ryan Speedo Green, bass-baritone, and Adam Nielsen, piano.

23 THURSDAY

☼ 7:13 AM / 5:03 PM

English opens at the Todd Haimes Theatre.

24 FRIDAY

☼ 7:12 AM / 5:04 PM

Martin Lawrence: Y'all Know What It Is! tour at Barclays Center

25 SATURDAY

☼ 7:11 AM / 5:05 PM

Comedian Nick Swardson at the Town Hall

26 SUNDAY

☼ 7:10 AM / 5:06 PM

The New York Travel and Adventure Show at Javits Center (and 25th)

● Jan. 27–Feb. 2

"We all talked a great deal about scale in New York. . . . We were happy to be in a city the beauty of which was unknown, uncozy, and not small scale."
 —Edwin Denby

27 MONDAY
7:10 AM / 5:07 PM

International Holocaust Remembrance Day

The Winter Show (Jan. 24–Feb. 2)

28 TUESDAY
7:09 AM / 5:09 PM

Les Arts Florissants, Zankel Hall Center Stage, Carnegie Hall

29 WEDNESDAY
7:08 AM / 5:10 PM   ● NEW MOON

Lunar New Year

Beatrice Rana plays Mendelssohn with the New York Philharmonic (through Feb. 2).

30 THURSDAY
☼ 7:07 AM / 5:11 PM

New York City Ballet presents *New Combinations* (and Jan. 29, 31, Feb. 2).

31 FRIDAY
☼ 7:06 AM / 5:12 PM

Piaf! Le Spectacle at the Town Hall

1 SATURDAY
☼ 7:05 AM / 5:14 PM

New York City Ballet presents *All Balanchine I* (and Jan. 21, 23, 25).

2 SUNDAY
☼ 7:04 AM / 5:15 PM

Groundhog Day

Last chance to see *Robert Caro's "The Power Broker" at 50* at the New-York Historical Society

FEBRUARY

EXCITEMENT AND DREAD, hope and anxiety. New Yorkers know the familiar feeling of awaiting the special chaos of a city snowstorm. Sanitation workers and school administrators stand at the ready, while kids and parents anxiously await the snow-day call (usually for opposite reasons), and every mayor since John Lindsay fears anything more than a few flakes—since nothing can undo a perfectly good mayoralty like a poorly managed storm. But few can deny the charming calm that descends on the bustling city brought to a standstill by mounds of fluffy white stuff, for a few hours anyway—bringing out the whimsy in even the most hard-as-nails New Yorkers. The **Metropolitan Museum of Art** opens *Caspar David Friedrich: The Soul of Nature* and it's your last chance to see *Edges of Ailey* at the **Whitney.**

PROFESSOR VATICINATE SAYS, *you're naive if you believe a groundhog's guess . . . but we think these first two weeks of February will see significant amounts of snow. It's snow fun for kids and sno' fun for adults. Snowflakes are a form of precipitation that goes from lovely to shovely. For Presidents' Day weekend it finally clears, then, believe it or not, it's another opening of another snow. It's also flu season: the "hoarse" and buggy days.*

NORMALS FOR
CENTRAL PARK

Avg. high: 42.2°
Avg. low: 29.5°
Avg. rainfall: 3.19"
Avg. snowfall: 10.1"

February 5 is National Weatherperson's Day. It is observed primarily here in the United States and recognizes/honors the men and women in the fields of meteorology, weather forecasting, and broadcast meteorology, as well as volunteer storm spotters and observers. It is commemorated on the birthday of John Jeffries, one of the United States' first weather observers, who took daily measurements from 1774 to 1816.

Sky Watch: Dazzling Venus and a waxing crescent Moon create an eye-catching celestial tableau at dusk in the west-southwest sky on the 1st. On the 6th, the gibbous Moon passes to the upper left of Jupiter. Venus reaches the pinnacle of its great brilliance on the 15th. It shines like a silvery beacon in the west-southwest for nearly 3.5 hours after sunset. Examine it with a telescope or even steadily held binoculars and you'll see it resembling a slender crescent Moon.

ANNALS OF THE NIGHT SKY

If you have an interest in astronomy, you might want to join the Amateur Observers' Society of New York, which celebrates its sixtieth viewing anniversary in 2025. This organization offers several options for viewing the sky, including its own observatory in the town of Southold, New York. Members also receive discounts on astronomy books, magazines, and telescopes.

NYC BOOK OF THE MONTH
Mott Street by Ava Chin (2023)

Chin uses her memoir as a jumping-off point to tell the long story of Chinese people in America. The story unfolds when she meets her father for the first time on a "cold, rainy late afternoon in mid-February" near Mott Street, where "hairdressers were busy fashioning buzz cuts" and "a crowd of tourists" enters "the city's first xiao long bao joint."

NYC MOVIE OF THE MONTH
Eternal Sunshine of the Spotless Mind, directed by Michel Gondry, starring Jim Carrey, Kate Winslet, and Tom Wilkinson (2004)

The film's bewitching premise—that it's possible to erase painful memories of lost love from the mind itself—means much of the action takes place inside Joel's head. But the lovers, Joel and Clementine, are New Yorkers, and the pivotal scene when Joel realizes Clementine has no idea who he is was shot at Columbia University Bookstore.

February has 28 days.

Feb. 3–9

"Miss Manhattan . . . is too self-sufficient, snobbish, and opinionated to be messing around with a Humphrey Bogart character like Brooklyn."
—Anita Loos

3 MONDAY

☼ 7:03 AM / 5:16 PM

1894: Norman Rockwell is born at West 103rd St.

4 TUESDAY

☼ 7:02 AM / 5:17 PM

New York City Ballet presents *All Stravinsky* (and Jan. 22, 24, 26, 28, Feb. 1).

5 WEDNESDAY

☼ 7:01 AM / 5:19 PM ☽ 1ST QUARTER

City Center Encores! presents *Urinetown* (through Feb. 16).

6 THURSDAY

●

☼ 7:00 AM / 5:20 PM

New York City Ballet presents *Innovators and Icons* (through Feb. 9).

7 FRIDAY

☼ 6:59 AM / 5:21 PM

Carnegie Hall presents the New York Pops' Let's Misbehave: The Songs of Cole Porter.

8 SATURDAY

☼ 6:58 AM / 5:22 PM

Caspar David Friedrich: The Soul of Nature opens at the Metropolitan Museum of Art (through May 11).

9 SUNDAY

☼ 6:56 AM / 5:23 PM

Last chance to see *Flow States: LA TRIENAL 2024* at El Museo del Barrio

 Feb. 10–16

he city is . . . a fountain that
ever stops."
— David Byrne

13 THURSDAY

☼ 6:52 AM / 5:28 PM

Karina Canellakis conducts Messiaen
and Debussy's *La Mer* at the New York
Philharmonic (through Feb. 18).

0 MONDAY

☼ 6:55 AM / 5:25 PM

81: *Des Refusés*, Keith Haring's first
olo exhibition, opens at Westbeth
ainters Space.

14 FRIDAY

☼ 6:50 AM / 5:30 PM

Valentine's Day

Pop the question, get hitched, or renew
your vows at the annual Love in Times
Square event.

1 TUESDAY

☼ 6:54 AM / 5:26 PM

unar New Year celebration at the
ew York Philharmonic

15 SATURDAY

☼ 6:49 AM / 5:31 PM

Susan B. Anthony's Birthday

Jazz at Lincoln Center presents
Dianne Reeves: With Love
(and 14th).

2 WEDNESDAY

☼ 6:53 AM / 5:27 PM   ○ FULL MOON

incoln's Birthday

New York City Ballet presents
alanchine + Wheeldon (and Feb. 14–16).

16 SUNDAY

☼ 6:48 AM / 5:32 PM

1976: Liz Smith's first gossip column is
published in the *New York Daily News*.

Feb. 17–23

"I like to think of all the city microcosms so nicely synchronized though unaware of one another."
—A. J. Liebling

17 MONDAY

☼ 6:46 AM / 5:33 PM

Presidents' Day

NYC Public Schools' Midwinter Recess begins (through Feb. 21).

18 TUESDAY

☼ 6:45 AM / 5:34 PM ♓ PISCES

New York City Ballet presents *All Balanchine II* (and Feb. 5, 8, 11, 13).

19 WEDNESDAY

☼ 6:44 AM / 5:36 PM

New York City Ballet performs *Swan Lake* (and Feb. 20–23, 25–28, Mar. 1–2).

20 THURSDAY

☼ 6:42 AM / 5:37 PM

☽ 3RD QUARTER

eMeLe-K, a weeklong celebration of MLK's legacy and the lasting contributions of Afro-Latinos, cocurated by Teatro LATEA and The Clemente (through Feb. 26).

21 FRIDAY

☼ 6:41 AM / 5:38 PM

Jazz at Lincoln Center presents Blues Jam (and 22nd).

22 SATURDAY

☼ 6:39 AM / 5:39 PM

Last chance to see *Vital Signs: Artists and the Body* at MoMA

23 SUNDAY

☼ 6:38 AM / 5:40 PM

Aerosmith: Peace Out, The Farewell Tour with the Black Crowes at Madison Square Garden

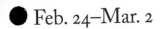 Feb. 24–Mar. 2

"People come here and they *want* things."
—Candace Bushnell

24 MONDAY

☼ 6:36 AM / 5:41 PM

1926: Florence Mills performs at Aeolian Hall.

25 TUESDAY

☼ 6:35 AM / 5:43 PM

The North Film Festival (through Feb. 28)

26 WEDNESDAY

☼ 6:34 AM / 5:44 PM

1989: Bill Cunningham's first official "Evening Hours" and "On the Street" columns are published in the *New York Times*.

27 THURSDAY

☼ 6:32 AM / 5:45 PM ● NEW MOON

Outsider Art Fair opens (through Mar. 2).

28 FRIDAY

☼ 6:30 AM / 5:46 PM

Gifts of Art in Honor of the 200th, *Brooklyn Made*, and *Building the Brooklyn Museum and Its Collection* open at the Brooklyn Museum.

1 SATURDAY

☼ 6:29 AM / 5:47 PM

Ramadan begins.

Journey Through Jazz Part VII at Jazz at Lincoln Center (and Feb. 28)

2 SUNDAY

☼ 6:27 AM / 5:48 PM

The Lord of the Rings in Concert: *The Return of the King* at Radio City Music Hall (and Feb. 27–28, Mar. 1)

MARCH

New York is a city that embraces the gutsy outsider—cunning, adaptable, fearless. Someone who is, as E. B. White wrote, "willing to be lucky." But the city can also be cruel to those who love it most—and "making it" is never guaranteed. So it was with Flaco, the Eurasian eagle-owl who escaped from the Central Park Zoo, spending a year incongruously swooping around the cityscape and perching on urban aeries—from water towers to fire escapes—before striking a building, weakened by rat poison. **Celebrate Flaco's birthday** (officially on the 15th) this month, and honor "a bird that flew free in a city that survives and flourishes despite all the challenges and attempts to stifle its spirit," as Zeynep Tufekci put it in the *Times*.

Professor Vaticinate says, *a sunny start to the month, then a slide to white, wet, and raw. For the second week of March, lionlike weather arrives: cloudy, then wild and rowdy. The Moon eclipse might be eclipsed by clouds. At midmonth, it's wet snow and rain up to your craw, followed by a sunny thaw. With spring's impending arrival, gardeners head outside to get the story on their lawns, and hope the plot thickens. The month comes to a close with rains so heavy you'll drown your Chevy.*

Normals for
Central Park
Avg. high: 49.9°
Avg. low: 35.8°
Avg. rainfall: 4.29"
Avg. snowfall: 5.0"

The Saint Patrick's Day Parade is one of New York City's greatest traditions. The first parade was on March 17, 1762—fourteen years before the signing of the Declaration of Independence. One might wonder how the weather has varied on parade day. Records going back to 1870 indicate that measurable snow has occurred just eight times, with the heaviest (3") in 1967. A year later was the rainiest day (1.42"). The coldest Saint Patrick's Day was in 1916 (+9°); the warmest was in 1945 (75°).

Sky Watch: One of nature's most beautiful and colorful shows will be performed during the predawn hours of the 14th: a total lunar eclipse. The Moon will enter the Earth's dark shadow (the umbra) at 1:09 a.m. Totality begins at 2:25 a.m. and will last for sixty-six minutes. The Moon will completely exit the umbra at 4:48 a.m.

ANNALS OF THE NIGHT SKY

At nightfall, look to the northeast to see the Big Dipper that will appear to be standing upright on its handle. When you see it, be sure to look for an incredible illusion. Just try to imagine eleven full Moons lined up between the two outer stars in the bowl—the so-called "Pointer stars," Dubhe and Merak. The Moon is half a degree wide and the Pointers are just over five degrees apart, so there's ample room. Now look again at the Big Dipper. Certainly, four moons would fit, maybe even five, but eleven?

NYC BOOK OF THE MONTH
Harriet the Spy by Louise Fitzhugh (1964)

In *Harriet the Spy*, an Upper West Side tomboy "spies" on the denizens of her school and neighborhood, writing cutting observations in her notebook. Fitzhugh—herself a queer denizen of 1950s Greenwich Village—created a character whose rebellion against the expected gender norms of tea parties, dance lessons, and class hierarchy was, and still is, subtly radical.

NYC MOVIE OF THE MONTH
The Muppets Take Manhattan, directed by Frank Oz, starring Jim Henson, Frank Oz, and Dave Goelz (1984)

This madcap tale of beloved puppets just trying to "put on a show" under the bright lights of Broadway is a send-up of a classic genre. It was filmed on location at spots like Central Park and Sardi's on 44th Street, and at Empire Stages in Long Island City where sets were constructed using a false floor to accommodate the hidden puppeteers.

March has 31 days.

Mar. 3–9

"You can't stop the monster, the city of New York, the hungry giant, looking for land and sky and space."
— Jami Attenberg

3 MONDAY

☼ 6:26 AM / 5:49 PM

1964: Police shut down a screening of Jack Smith's *Flaming Creatures* at the New Bowery Theatre and arrest Jonas Mekas, Kenneth Jacobs, and Florence Karpf.

4 TUESDAY

☼ 6:24 AM / 5:51 PM

Metropolitan Opera presents *Fidelio* (through Mar. 15).

5 WEDNESDAY

☼ 6:23 AM / 5:52 PM

Ash Wednesday

Carnegie Hall presents London Symphony Orchestra (and 6th).

6 THURSDAY

☼ 6:21 AM / 5:53 PM

◑ 1ST QUARTER

City Center presents *Flamenco Festival* (through Mar. 9).

7 FRIDAY

6:20 AM / 5:54 PM

The Book of Esther in the Age of Rembrandt opens at the Jewish Museum (through Aug. 10).

8 SATURDAY

6:18 AM / 5:55 PM

International Women's Day

New York Philharmonic presents Young People's Concert: The Future Is Female.

9 SUNDAY

☼ 7:16 AM / 6:56 PM

Daylight saving time begins.

Last chance to see *Harmony and Dissonance: Orphism in Paris, 1910–1930* at the Guggenheim.

● Mar. 10–16

"In the New York days of my twenties, the streets were wide open and always sunny, not narrow and closed and dark, the way they are now."
—Jamaica Kincaid

10 MONDAY

☼ 7:15 AM / 6:57 PM

New York International Children's Film Festival (Mar. 2–16)

11 TUESDAY

☼ 7:13 AM / 6:58 PM

Metropolitan Opera presents a new production of *Moby-Dick* (Mar. 3–29).

12 WEDNESDAY

☼ 7:12 AM / 6:59 PM

City Center presents *Twyla Tharp Dance* (through Mar. 15).

13 THURSDAY

☼ 7:10 AM / 7:00 PM

Puerto Rico in Print: The Posters of Lorenzo Homar opens at the Poster House (through Sep. 7).

14 FRIDAY

☼ 7:08 AM / 7:02 PM   ○ FULL MOON

Purim

Jazz at Lincoln Center presents Anat Cohen: Journeys, a 50th Birthday Celebration in the Appel Room (and 15th).

15 SATURDAY

☼ 7:07 AM / 7:03 PM

Gustavo Dudamel takes the podium for the first time as the New York Philharmonic's new music and artistic director (Mar. 13–16).

16 SUNDAY

☼ 7:08 AM / 7:04 PM

Last chance to see *Barbie: A Cultural Icon* at the Museum of Arts and Design

Mar. 17–23

"Anyone who has been confronted by a rat in the bleakness of a Manhattan dawn and has seen it whirl and slink away, understands fully why this beast has been for centuries a symbol of the Judas."
—Joseph Mitchell

17 MONDAY

☼ 7:03 AM / 7:05 PM

Saint Patrick's Day

Saint Patrick's Day Parade, Fifth Ave.

18 TUESDAY

☼ 7:02 AM / 7:06 PM

Carnegie Hall hosts the Cleveland Orchestra (and 19th).

19 WEDNESDAY

☼ 7:00 AM / 7:07 PM

New York Philharmonic presents *Back to the Future* in Concert (through Mar. 22).

20 THURSDAY

☼ 6:58 AM / 7:09 PM   ♈ARIES

Vernal Equinox

1948: The Photo League, a cooperative founded by Sol Libsohn and Sid Grossman in 1936, is blacklisted as subversive.

21 FRIDAY

☼ 6:57 AM / 7:09 PM

1964: The Huntington Hartford Gallery of Modern Art opens in an Edward Durell Stone–designed building at Columbus Circle.

22 SATURDAY

☼ 6:55 AM / 7:10 PM   ◑ 3RD QUARTER

Katt Williams: Heaven on Earth tour at Barclays Center

23 SUNDAY

☼ 6:53 AM / 7:11 PM

Last chance to see *Samurai Splendor: Sword Fittings from Edo Japan* at the Met

● Mar. 24–30

"In New York . . . I feel up against the sublime. The substance of life, in all its stimulating potential or grimness, grandeur, and folly, is conveyed to me by these very streets."

—Phillip Lopate

24 MONDAY

☿ 6:52 AM / 7:12 PM

1900: Mayor Robert Anderson Van Wyck breaks ground on the New York City Subway system in front of City Hall, named "Tunnel Day."

25 TUESDAY

☿ 6:50 AM / 7:13 PM

Manhattan Theatre Club presents the Broadway premiere of *Stephen Sondheim's Old Friends* with Bernadette Peters and Lea Salonga at the Samuel Friedman Theatre.

26 WEDNESDAY

☿ 6:48 AM / 7:14 PM

Lailat al-Qadr

City Center Encores! presents *Love Life* (through Mar. 30).

27 THURSDAY

☿ 6:47 AM / 7:15 PM

1964: A flawed report in the *New York Times* about the murder of Kitty Genovese fosters the idea of urban apathy and indifference.

28 FRIDAY

☿ 6:45 AM / 7:16 PM

The IFPDA Print Fair at the Park Ave. Armory (preview Mar. 27, through Mar. 30)

29 SATURDAY

☿ 6:44 AM / 7:17 PM ● NEW MOON

Leonard Slatkin conducts Shostakovich's Fifth, New York Philharmonic (begins Mar. 26).

30 SUNDAY

☿ 6:42 AM / 7:19 PM

Ramadan ends.

Last chance to see *Draw Them In, Paint Them Out: Trenton Doyle Hancock Confronts Philip Guston* at the Jewish Museum

Mar. 31–Apr. 6

"You begin to map yourself to the city even as the city itself is always changing in front of you and beneath you and above you."
—Colin Harrison

31 MONDAY

☼ 6:40 AM / 7:20 PM

Eid al-Fitr

Metropolitan Opera presents *Le Nozze di Figaro* (through May 17).

1 TUESDAY

☼ 6:39 AM / 7:21 PM

April Fool's Day

1981: The *Absurdities* show, organized by Robert Goldman, opens at ABC No Rio on the Lower East Side.

2 WEDNESDAY

☼ 6:37 AM / 7:22 PM

Standard Time with Michael Feinstein, Carnegie Hall Big Band

3 THURSDAY ●

☼ 6:35 AM / 7:23 PM

City Center presents *Sara Mearns: Artists at the Center* (through Apr. 5).

4 FRIDAY

☼ 6:34 AM / 7:24 PM ☽ 1ST QUARTER

Jazz at Lincoln Center presents The Real Ambassadors: Armstrong and Brubeck in the Appel Room (and 5th)

5 SATURDAY

☼ 6:32 AM / 7:25 PM

New York City Tartan Day Parade

6 SUNDAY

☼ 6:30 AM / 7:26 PM

New York International Antiquarian Book Fair (Apr. 3–6)

APRIL

HIGH FASHION, HIGH ART, HIGH LINE. Before the former freight railway was erected in 1934, the trains running along Eleventh Avenue at street level were so dangerous that the so-called "West Side Cowboys of Death Avenue" cleared pedestrians from the tracks. Although today the **High Line** is more like a tourist superhighway in the sky, if you stroll it as springtime flowers bloom—before it gets too hot to bother—it's a great way to be alone in a crowd. **Dip into the galleries** in the 20s, or stop at the **Brass Monkey** for a cold beer at a spot that's been there since *before*. Or, let the art come to you. In honor of its 200th birthday, the **Brooklyn Museum is launching Museum on Wheels**, an interactive art and education experience bringing cultural programming throughout the borough.

PROFESSOR VATICINATE SAYS, *no fooling! Here comes the Sun. It warms our buns. But then, an abrupt shift back to rain/sleet and maybe even wet snow. Oh winter, please go away! We're sick of you, it's too cold to play. Midmonth could see a rumble of thunder, then . . . what's this? Are unsettled conditions easing . . . or is it teasing? We think you'll need shade for the Easter Parade. Then flowers bloom as more showers loom, followed by rain by the bucketful as the month ends.*

NORMALS FOR
CENTRAL PARK

Avg. high: 61.8°
Avg. low: 45.5°
Avg. rainfall: 4.09"
Avg. snowfall: 0.4"

Sixty years ago, NYC was experiencing a severe drought. The year 1965 holds the record for having less than thirty inches of precipitation (26.09" was measured, about twenty inches below average). Reservoir levels hit an all-time low of 24.8 percent of capacity. Strict water conservation rulings were issued, including closing public pools and prohibiting watering of lawns. Even Tiffany's did its part, substituting the water in its fountains with gin, thus saving sixteen gallons!

Sky Watch: Venus, which transitioned into the morning sky on March 22, again reaches its peak brilliance on the 28th. Look for it low near the eastern horizon around 5 a.m. Situated to its lower right is much-dimmer Saturn; if you want to see Saturn's rings through a telescope, you'll be disappointed, as they are now turned edgewise to Earth. A curve extended from the arc of the Big Dipper's handle leads to the brightest star of spring, orange Arcturus.

ANNALS OF THE NIGHT SKY

To determine the date of Easter in a given year, the rule of thumb is that it occurs on the first Sunday after the first full Moon of spring (the Paschal Moon). This year's Paschal Moon comes on Saturday, the 12th, but Easter Sunday arrives on the following Sunday, the 20th. The reason is that for Europe—and the Vatican—the Paschal Moon occurs after midnight on Sunday, the 13th, thus delaying Easter for a full week.

NYC BOOK OF THE MONTH
Pineapple Street: A Novel by Jenny Jackson (2023)

Literary editor Jenny Jackson's debut is a portrait of the monied "fruit streets" of Brooklyn Heights, an enclave whose ethos is summed up in a coffee shop under the "watery April sun" when a character exclaims, "Oh no! I left my Cartier bracelet in Lena's BMW and she's leaving soon for her grandmother's house in Southampton!"

NYC MOVIE OF THE MONTH
Tootsie, directed by Sydney Pollack, starring Dustin Hoffman, Bill Murray, Jessica Lange, and Teri Garr (1982)

Hoffman's commitment to the role of Michael Dorsey—an unemployable, neurotic New York City actor who transforms into Dorothy Michaels, a hardworking soap opera star—gives poignancy to a film that might otherwise be pure farce. As critic A. O. Scott said, "Hoffman plays Michael straight, which is how Michael plays Dorothy."

April has 30 days.

 Apr. 7–13

If your head is down, you walk
into people. You keep your head
up, like you own the street."
—Whoopi Goldberg

7 MONDAY

☼ 6:29 AM / 7:27 PM

Metropolitan Opera presents *Die
Zauberflöte* (Mar. 23–Apr. 26).

8 TUESDAY

☼ 6:27 AM / 7:28 PM

Last chance to see *The Great Hall
Commission: Tong Yang-Tze* at
the Met

9 WEDNESDAY

☼ 6:26 AM / 7:29 PM

New York Philharmonic performs
*Brahms, Stravinsky, and Jessie
Montgomery* (through Apr. 11).

10 THURSDAY

☼ 6:24 AM / 7:30 PM

City Center presents Dance Theatre
of Harlem (through Apr. 13).

11 FRIDAY

☼ 6:23 AM / 7:31 PM

Carnegie Hall presents Arturo
O'Farrill and the Afro Latin Jazz
Orchestra.

12 SATURDAY

☼ 6:21 AM / 7:32 PM   ○ FULL MOON

Passover begins.

Barnyard Egg Hunt at Queens County
Farm Museum (and Apr. 19)

13 SUNDAY

☼ 6:19 AM / 7:33 PM

Palm Sunday

Last chance to see *Franz Kafka* at the
Morgan Library and Museum

Apr. 14–20

"New York, too often, has looked across the sea toward Europe. And all of us who turn our eyes away from what we have are missing life."
—Norman Rockwell

14 MONDAY
☼ 6:18 AM / 7:34 PM

NYC Public Schools' Spring Recess begins (through Apr. 18).

15 TUESDAY
☼ 6:16 AM / 7:35 PM

Tax Day

MLB celebrates Jackie Robinson Day.

16 WEDNESDAY
☼ 6:15 AM / 7:36 PM

1993: The city's first Critical Mass bike ride meets at Washington Square Park.

17 THURSDAY ●
☼ 6:13 AM / 7:37 PM

1951: Mickey Mantle's first game as a New York Yankee, Yankee Stadium

18 FRIDAY
☼ 6:12 AM / 7:38 PM

Good Friday

Jazz at Lincoln Center presents Paquito D'Rivera: Celebrating 70+ Years in Music (and 19th).

19 SATURDAY
☼ 6:10 AM / 7:39 PM ♉ TAURUS

Celebrate Open Streets: Car-Free Earth Day at locations throughout the five boroughs.

20 SUNDAY
☼ 6:09 AM / 7:40 PM ☽ 3RD QUARTER

Easter Sunday
Passover ends.

Easter Bonnet Parade outside Saint Patrick's Cathedral

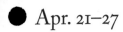 Apr. 21–27

"I must wait for a shower of shil-
lings, or at least a slight dew
or mizzling of sixpences, before I
explore New York very far."
—Henry David Thoreau

21 MONDAY

☿ 6:07 AM / 7:42 PM

Metropolitan Opera presents *Il
Barbiere di Siviglia* (Apr. 15–Jun. 5).

22 TUESDAY

☿ 6:06 AM / 7:43 PM

Earth Day

Day of service at Queens County
Farm Museum

23 WEDNESDAY

☿ 6:05 AM / 7:44 PM

New York International Auto Show at
Javits Center (Apr. 18–27)

24 THURSDAY

☿ 6:03 AM / 7:45 PM

The Pirates of Penzance opens at the
Todd Haimes Theatre.

25 FRIDAY

☿ 6:02 AM / 7:46 PM

Arbor Day

New York Philharmonic presents
Mozart and "The Wooden Prince"
(through Apr. 27).

26 SATURDAY

☿ 6:00 AM / 7:47 PM

1895: New York Zoological Society
is chartered (renamed the Wildlife
Conservation Society in 1993).

27 SUNDAY

☿ 5:59 AM / 7:48 PM ● NEW MOON

NYCRUNS Brooklyn Half Marathon

Apr. 28–May 4

"New York is not, on the whole, the best place to enjoy the downright miraculous nature of the planet."
—Loren Eiseley, 1957

28 MONDAY

☼ 5:58 AM / 7:49 PM

1990: *A Chorus Line* closes at the Shubert Theatre after 6,137 performances.

29 TUESDAY

☼ 5:56 AM / 7:50 PM

Celebrate Poem in Your Pocket Day with a verse by Langston Hughes or Edna St. Vincent Millay.

30 WEDNESDAY

☼ 5:55 AM / 7:51 PM

City Center Encores! presents *The Wild Party* (through May 11).

1 THURSDAY

●

☼ 5:54 AM / 7:52 PM

1938: The *Harvard Lampoon* parodies *Vogue* with articles like "Drip and Drool from the Flushing Openings" and "Nicotine is Nice: A Study of Cigarette Society."

2 FRIDAY

☼ 5:53 AM / 7:53 PM

Jazz at Lincoln Center presents Christian McBride and Ursa Major (and 3rd).

3 SATURDAY

☼ 5:51 AM / 7:54 PM

Carnegie Hall presents Kurt Rosenwinkel, guitar.

4 SUNDAY

☼ 5:50 AM / 7:55 PM ◐ 1ST QUARTER

TD Five Boro Bike Tour

MAY

LAZING IN A PATCH of sunlight on a scuffed green-and-white linoleum floor, batting at ATM users, lounging on a stack of the *New York Post,* or peering out from behind dusty canned vegetables on a low shelf, the bodega cat is as much a New Yorker as the most pampered Upper East Side pup—bodega cats even have more than one adoring Instagram account following their every move. This month, join the **Municipal Art Society for a Jane's Walk** in honor of urbanist Jane Jacobs' birthday, or take part in **AIDS Walk New York** to raise money and awareness. Visit Marsha P. Johnson State Park in Williamsburg to celebrate **Trans Day of Visibility**, and catch **Christian McBride performing at Jazz at Lincoln Center.**

PROFESSOR VATICINATE SAYS, *bright but brisk as May begins. Then . . . for a while . . . it's hot as hell, so kick off your shoes and sweat a spell. Humidity is what heat uses for an alibi, and during May's second week, you'll need a sense of humid, for squally storms are rumored. May's third week is brilliant, but still, you'd better be resilient . . . and "water repillient!" A protracted spell of nice weather finally moves in, but will it arrive in time for the holiday?*

NORMALS FOR
CENTRAL PARK
Avg. high: 71.4°
Avg. low: 55.0°
Avg. rainfall: 3.96"

According to the official records of the National Weather Service, dating back to 1869, it has snowed in May in NYC only twice, in 1977 and 2020; both times on the same date, the 9th. Each time only a "trace" of snow was noted. But according to weather historian David Ludlam, on May 8, 1803, "a considerable fall of snow" occurred in NYC. The occasion was made memorable by the appearance of sleighs in the Hudson Valley, with "snow several inches deep" in Poughkeepsie!

Sky Watch: On the 3rd, take note of Mars, sitting just below the Moon. Mars has now receded more than seventy-five million miles from Earth since it was closest to us in mid-January, and appears about one-third as bright. On the evenings of the 4th and 5th, using binoculars, you can see Mars passing through a splattering of faint stars known as the Beehive Star Cluster.

ANNALS OF THE NIGHT SKY

Fifty years ago, NYC skywatchers were disappointed when a long-awaited total eclipse of the Moon was scheduled on the Saturday night of Memorial Day weekend. The local forecast promised "fair skies," but just as the celestial show was about to get underway, a cold front dropped south from New England, blanketing the tristate area with clouds and scattered thunderstorms.

NYC BOOK OF THE MONTH
Red at the Bone by Jacqueline Woodson (2019)

Woodson's novel opens on "the last day in May" as sixteen-year-old Melody, wearing a dress her mother never got to wear, descends the stairs of her grandparents' Brooklyn brownstone for her coming-of-age ceremony. The book traces the history of two families joined and separated by love, and is narrated in short pieces by each of the main characters.

NYC MOVIE OF THE MONTH
Party Girl, directed by Daisy von Scherler Mayer, starring Parker Posey, Omar Townsend, and The Lady Bunny (1995)

A movie where a downtown party girl saves herself by reluctantly becoming a librarian has an only-in-New York vibe. In one scene she reorganizes her roommate's records, complete with a card catalog, much to his chagrin. The film was Posey's first leading role—Mayer recalled being told, "There's this girl running around town with this great wardrobe. She is Mary."—and was the first film to be released on the internet.

May has 31 days.

 May 5–11

"Manhattan is the twentieth century's Rosetta Stone."
—Rem Koolhaas

5 MONDAY
☼ 5:49 AM / 7:56 PM

Cinco de Mayo

Metropolitan Museum of Art's Costume Institute Gala

6 TUESDAY
☼ 5:48 AM / 7:57 PM

Metropolitan Opera presents a new production of *Salome* (Apr. 29–May 24).

7 WEDNESDAY
☼ 5:47 AM / 7:58 PM

1974: Norman Mailer publishes *The Faith of Graffiti*, a defense of the art style's young artists.

8 THURSDAY
☼ 5:45 AM / 7:59 PM

New York City Ballet Spring Gala featuring *Vienna Waltzes*

9 FRIDAY
☼ 5:44 AM / 8:00 PM

TEFAF New York Art Fair opens (through May 13).

10 SATURDAY
☼ 5:43 AM / 8:01 PM

American Art Fair at Bohemian National Hall (through May 13)

11 SUNDAY
☼ 5:42 AM / 8:02 PM

Mother's Day

Last chance to see *Floridas: Anastasia Samoylova and Walker Evans* at the Met

May 12–18

"There is no city in the Union in which imposters of all kinds flourish so well as in New York."
—James D. McCabe, 1872

12 MONDAY

☼ 5:41 AM / 8:03 PM   ○ FULL MOON

Vesak

Metropolitan Opera presents *Antony and Cleopatra* (through Jun. 7).

13 TUESDAY

☼ 5:40 AM / 8:04 PM

New York City Ballet presents *Contemporary Choreography* (and May 10, 17, 23).

14 WEDNESDAY

☼ 5:39 AM / 8:05 PM

New York City Ballet performs *All Ravel* (and May 15, 18, 20, 22, 24).

15 THURSDAY

●

☼ 5:38 AM / 8:06 PM

1918: The first scheduled airmail service between Washington, DC, and NYC takes flight.

16 FRIDAY

☼ 5:37 AM / 8:07 PM

New York Philharmonic presents *Renée Fleming and Rod Gilfry Sing Kevin Puts* (through May 18).

17 SATURDAY

☼ 5:36 AM / 8:08 PM

Dance Parade and Festival

18 SUNDAY

☼ 5:36 AM / 8:09 PM

AIDS Walk New York

● May 19–25

> "One story is good only till another is told, and skyscrapers are the last word of economic ingenuity only till another word be written."
> —Henry James

19 MONDAY

☼ 5:35 AM / 8:10 PM

1983: Creative Time opens its first Art in the Anchorage program, celebrating the Brooklyn Bridge centennial with performances and installations inside the bridge's anchorage.

20 TUESDAY

☼ 5:34 AM / 8:11 PM   ◑ 3RD QUARTER
♊ GEMINI

1926: Humphrey Bogart marries Helen Menken in New York—they divorce on November 18, 1927.

21 WEDNESDAY

☼ 5:33 AM / 8:12 PM

Fleet Week begins (through May 27).

22 THURSDAY

☼ 5:32 AM / 8:13 PM

Carnegie Hall presents Cimafunk and La Tribu.

23 FRIDAY

☼ 5:32 AM / 8:14 PM

Metropolitan Opera presents *The Queen of Spades* (through Jun. 7).

24 SATURDAY

☼ 5:31 AM / 8:14 PM

1870: Supreme Court Justice Benjamin Cardozo is born in New York.

25 SUNDAY

☼ 5:30 AM / 8:15 PM

Last chance to see *Somewhere to Roost* at the American Folk Art Museum

May 26–Jun. 1

"Every man Jack when he first sets foot on the stones of Manhattan has got to fight.... It is slugging from the first. It is a fight to a finish."
   —O. Henry

26 MONDAY

☼ 5:30 AM / 8:16 PM ● NEW MOON

Memorial Day

Celebrate Memorial Day with parades in Bay Ridge and Little Neck Douglaston, or at the Intrepid Museum.

27 TUESDAY

☼ 5:29 AM / 8:17 PM

Last chance to see *The Façade Commission: Lee Bul* at the Met

28 WEDNESDAY

☼ 5:28 AM / 8:18 PM

New York City Ballet presents *A Midsummer Night's Dream* (and May 27, 29–31, Jun. 1).

29 THURSDAY

☼ 5:28 AM / 8:19 PM

Ascension Day

Ballet Hispánico at City Center (through Jun. 1).

30 FRIDAY

☼ 5:27 AM / 8:19 PM

The Brooklyn Film Festival celebrates its twenty-eighth edition in Brooklyn and online (through Jun. 8).

31 SATURDAY

☼ 5:27 AM / 8:20 PM

Casita Maria celebrates its ninetieth anniversary with the South Bronx Culture Festival: Born in El Barrio and Raised in the South Bronx (May 30 through Jun. 1).

1 SUNDAY

☼ 5:27 AM / 8:21 PM

Shavuot begins.

Gustavo Dudamel leads Mahler's Seventh with the New York Philharmonic (begins May 27).

JUNE

WHAT BETTER PLACE to observe what Jane Jacobs called "the ballet of the good city sidewalk" than sitting on a stoop. The city's stoops—from the Upper East Side to Crown Heights—owe their origin to the Dutch practice of building living spaces above street level, and the city's lack of alleys. They are liminal spaces—in, but not of, the street life of the sidewalk. Photographer Helen Levitt found kids playing and adults chewing the fat on stoops in the 1930s and '40s, while the stoop is almost a character in Spike Lee's 1989 film *Do the Right Thing*. During the pandemic, stoops gave New Yorkers a safe place to be outside together. As summer kicks off, it's a perfect spot to take in a **block party**. This month, be sure to check out events like **Juneteeth**, the **Pride March**, and the **Schomburg Center Literary Festival**.

PROFESSOR VATICINATE SAYS, *June is here and the living turns easy: balmy and breezy. We forecast a dry track for the Belmont Stakes. Thereafter, a last sunny glimpse, followed by a hard rinse. Midmonth is fine and pleasant; for bride s it's auspicious, even propitious. Just as summer officially arrives, Thor's hammer will clammer. Then, as the month winds down, rub your eyes . . . sunny skies! It's azure thing.*

NORMALS FOR
CENTRAL PARK
Avg. high: 79.7°
Avg. low: 64.4°
Avg. rainfall: 4.54"

The 2025 hurricane season officially begins on the 1st. Ninety years ago, one of the most intense Atlantic hurricanes on record made landfall in the U.S. Known in weather annals as the 1935 Labor Day Hurricane, it wrought tremendous damage to the Florida Keys, producing a storm surge up to twenty feet high. Highest winds reached 185 mph, while the barometric pressure fell to 26.34", the lowest ever recorded in the U.S.

SKY WATCH: The full Moon of the 11th takes an unusually low track across the southern sky. Since objects seen low in the sky are affected by the reddening properties of the atmosphere, June's full Moon usually has a beautiful golden appearance (the "Honey Moon"). At nightfall on the 29th, look west to see Mars positioned just above a crescent Moon. The Summer Star Triangle of Deneb, Vega, and Altair are displayed low in the east.

ANNALS OF THE NIGHT SKY

In 1991, mathematician Dr. Alexander Abian made a wild suggestion to the U.S. government: that we blow up the Moon! He claimed that a moonless Earth wouldn't wobble, eradicating the seasons and, in consequence, heat waves, snowstorms, and hurricanes. In response, astronomer Sir Patrick Moore described this idea and its proposer as "NAFC!" (nutty as a fruitcake).

NYC BOOK OF THE MONTH
Harlem Shuffle by Colson Whitehead (2021)

Harlem furniture store owner Ray Carney is trying to stay on the right side of the law, while not asking too many questions, when "his cousin Freddie brought him on the heist one hot night in early June." The plan—to rob the famous Hotel Theresa, known in real life for hosting prominent Black people who were denied stays in the city's elite hotels—quickly goes awry in this novel of family ties and double lives set in the early 1960s.

NYC MOVIE OF THE MONTH
The Naked City, directed by Jules Dassin, starring Barry Fitzgerald, Howard Duff, and Dorothy Hart (1948)

This noir police procedural—opening with the murder of a beautiful blonde—owes its visual style to tabloid photographer Weegee, who was an adviser. As it opens, a narrator assures viewers it wasn't shot on a set, but "on the streets, in the apartment houses, in the skyscrapers, of New York itself," and that "a great many thousand" New Yorkers played themselves.

June has 30 days.

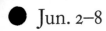 Jun. 2–8

"To some natures this stimulant of life in a great city becomes a thing as binding and necessary as opium is to one addicted to the habit."
—James Weldon Johnson

2 MONDAY

☼ 5:26 AM / 8:21 PM ◑ 1ST QUARTER

1897: Brooklyn Museum opens.

3 TUESDAY

☼ 5:26 AM / 8:22 PM

Shavuot ends.

MoMA's benefit Party in the Garden

4 WEDNESDAY

☼ 5:25 AM / 8:23 PM

1980: Coca Crystal interviews Dana Lobell of Women Against Pornography on her public access show, *If I Can't Dance, You Can Keep Your Revolution.*

5 THURSDAY

☼ 5:25 AM / 8:23 PM

New York City Independent Film Festival (and Jun. 3–4, 6–7)

6 FRIDAY

☼ 5:25 AM / 8:24 PM

D-Day

1998: *Sex and the City* debuts on HBO.

7 SATURDAY

☼ 5:25 AM / 8:25 PM

Eid al-Adha

1976: Amos Poe's *Unmade Beds*, starring Duncan Hannah, Patti Astor, and Debbie Harry, screens at 814 Broadway.

8 SUNDAY

☼ 5:24 AM / 8:25 PM

National Puerto Rican Day Parade

Jun. 9–15

"We were very tired, we were
    very merry—
We had gone back and forth all
    night on the ferry."
    —Edna St. Vincent Millay, 1919

9 MONDAY

☼ 5:24 AM / 8:26 PM

1937: Italy wins an international
boxing match against the U.S. at
Yankee Stadium in front of fifty-two
thousand fans—the last of its kind
before WWII.

10 TUESDAY

☼ 5:24 AM / 8:26 PM

New York "Sounds of Summer" Festival at Carnegie Hall (and Jun. 8-9, 11)

11 WEDNESDAY

☼ 5:24 AM / 8:27 PM   ○ FULL MOON

Star Wars: The Empire Strikes Back in
Concert, New York Philharmonic
(through Jun. 14)

12 THURSDAY

☼ 5:24 AM / 8:27 PM

Carnegie Hall presents the
Met Orchestra.

13 FRIDAY

☼ 5:24 AM / 8:28 PM

1940: Isabel Hoey, daughter of the
mayor of North Carolina, christens the
battleship *North Carolina* at Brooklyn
Navy Yard.

14 SATURDAY

☼ 5:24 AM / 8:28 PM

Flag Day

Flag Day Parade, starting at City Hall
Park and ending with celebrations at
Fraunces Tavern.

15 SUNDAY

☼ 5:24 AM / 8:29 PM

Father's Day

Harlem Skyscraper Cycling Classic
around Marcus Garvey Park

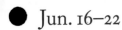 Jun. 16–22

"As I walk up Broadway, the people that brush past me seem always hastening toward a destination they will never reach."
—Helen Keller

16 MONDAY
☼ 5:24 AM / 8:29 PM

1937: *The Cradle Will Rock*, an anti-capitalist musical produced by the Federal Theater Project, is performed from Venice Theatre's seats after the WPA padlocked its Broadway theater.

17 TUESDAY
☼ 5:24 AM / 8:29 PM

Museum Mile Festival

18 WEDNESDAY
☼ 5:24 AM / 8:30 PM ◑ 3RD QUARTER

1910: President Theodore Roosevelt addresses crowds in NYC after an extended trip abroad.

19 THURSDAY
☼ 5:24 AM / 8:30 PM

Juneteenth

Celebrate Juneteenth at a festival in Crown Heights and Brownsville, Brooklyn.

20 FRIDAY
☼ 5:24 AM / 8:30 PM

Summer Solstice

Observe the summer solstice with yoga in Times Square.

21 SATURDAY
☼ 5:25 AM / 8:30 PM ♋ CANCER

Coney Island Mermaid Parade and Ball

22 SUNDAY
☼ 5:25 AM / 8:30 PM

Last chance to see *Real Clothes, Real Lives: 200 Years of What Women Wore, the Smith College Historic Clothing Collection* at the New-York Historical Society

Jun. 23–29

"At the foot of the buildings the revolving doors are whirling like crazy wheels, each fan blowing out human beings onto the sidewalks."
—Paul Morand, 1930

23 MONDAY

☼ 5:25 AM / 8:31 PM

1961: The American Folk Art Museum is founded.

24 TUESDAY

☼ 5:25 AM / 8:31 PM

1935: Journalist Pete Hamill is born in Brooklyn.

25 WEDNESDAY

☼ 5:26 AM / 8:31 PM ● NEW MOON

1937: Jacob Riis Park and Orchard Beach open.

26 THURSDAY

☼ 5:26 AM / 8:31 PM

Islamic New Year

Last day of school for NYC Public Schools

27 FRIDAY

☼ 5:27 AM / 8:31 PM

1951: New York Giants Ed Stanky is presented with a diamond-encrusted baseball bat by the Bowery Jeweler's Association.

28 SATURDAY

☼ 5:27 AM / 8:31 PM

Rainbows on the Hudson Pride boat parade

29 SUNDAY

☼ 5:27 AM / 8:31 PM

NYC Pride March

JULY

July's stagnant heat can make a city surrounded by water feel surprisingly landlocked. But lately the city has been chipping away at the barriers holding New Yorkers back from its 520 miles of waterfront (protected by fireboats since 1875). Take advantage of calming water views at **Brooklyn Bridge Park,** Long Island City's **Gantry Plaza State Park,** the Upper West Side's new **Waterline Square Park,** or Manhattan's first so-called **"beach" at Gansevoort Peninsula** (just don't actually try to *swim* in the Hudson River) where David Hammons' sculpture *Day's End* pays tribute to a time when the abandoned industrial waterfront was enjoyed by artists and other outsiders.

Professor Vaticinate says, *as July arrives, we deal initially with hit-or-miss showers, which, by the second week of the month, lead to dark clouds that glower . . . then watch as we cower in steady, heavy showers. Suddenly at midmonth, it turns torrid (some say horrid). You'll look at your electric bill for air-conditioning and lose your cool. July's third week is frequently thundery; an "enlightning" experience. A hot end to the month, so be wary of getting a sunburn; it's more than what you basked for.*

Normals for Central Park
Avg. high: 84.9°
Avg. low: 70.1°
Avg. rainfall: 4.60"

Since records have been kept at Central Park, dating back to 1869, two years are tied for the most days (39) that the temperature has reached or exceeded 90°. Interestingly, they both occurred within two years of each other: 1991 and 1993. In contrast, the year when the temperature hit or exceeded 90° the least number of times—just once—was back in 1902. On average, the temperature hits or exceeds 90° seventeen days a year at Central Park.

Sky Watch: Early morning of the 20th in the eastern sky, a crescent Moon will pass in front of the Pleiades star cluster; a beautiful sight as seen through binoculars. The first star to disappear behind the Moon's bright limb will be Electra at 4:37 a.m. The next morning, the eastern sky will be adorned by the Moon hanging directly above Venus. Earth is at aphelion (farthest from the Sun) at 4 p.m. on the 3rd, but the Northern Hemisphere is tilted toward the Sun, so we have hot weather.

ANNALS OF THE NIGHT SKY

The largest object currently circling Earth is the International Space Station (ISS). It's also the brightest, sometimes even rivaling Venus. For a specific schedule as to when it will be passing over your neighborhood, go to https://spotthestation.nasa.gov/.

NYC BOOK OF THE MONTH
The Fire Next Time by James Baldwin (1963)

In one of the two essays in this book—first published in the *New Yorker* as "Letter from a Region in my Mind"—Baldwin explores race, religion, and growing up in Harlem. He writes, "What I saw around me that summer in Harlem was what I had always seen; nothing had changed. But now, without any warning, the whores and pimps and racketeers on the Avenue had become a personal menace. It had not before occurred to me that I could become one of them."

NYC MOVIE OF THE MONTH
Rear Window, directed by Alfred Hitchcock, starring James Stewart, Grace Kelly, and Wendell Corey (1954)

Hitchcock's star spends his days in rapt attention to the goings-on of his neighbors, a pastime most New Yorkers can relate to. But the film—whose setting in a courtyard apartment is as important as its plot—was actually shot entirely in California at Paramount Studios. The enormous, complicated set was based on 125 Christopher Street in Greenwich Village.

July has 31 days.

 Jun. 30–Jul. 6

"Nothing will cut New York but
a diamond."
—Dawn Powell

30 MONDAY
☼ 5:28 AM / 8:31 PM

1938: President Franklin D. Roosevelt
visits the construction site for the
1939-40 World's Fair.

1 TUESDAY
☼ 5:28 AM / 8:31 PM

1939: Residents move into the Red
Hook Houses, a public housing devel-
opment in Brooklyn.

2 WEDNESDAY
☼ 5:29 AM / 8:30 PM ◑ 1ST QUARTER

1999: Spike Lee's *Summer of Sam* opens
in theaters.

3 THURSDAY
☼ 5:29 AM / 8:30 PM

1981: The *New York Times* first reports
on a mysterious illness that would later
be known as AIDS.

4 FRIDAY
☼ 5:30 AM / 8:30 PM

Independence Day

Nathan's Famous Hot Dog Eating
Contest at the corner of Surf and
Stillwell Aves., Coney Island

5 SATURDAY
☼ 5:31 AM / 8:30 PM

1989: *Seinfeld* debuts on NBC.

6 SUNDAY
☼ 5:31 AM / 8:29 PM

Last chance to see *Solid Gold* at the
Brooklyn Museum

Jul. 7–13

"Relief was sought ... at the fire hydrants that reckless boys opened with giant wrenches. The cold water made the black asphalt blacker in the black nights."
—Hilton Als

7 MONDAY

☼ 5:32 AM / 8:29 PM

1831: President James Monroe lies in state at City Hall for three days after his death.

8 TUESDAY

☼ 5:32 AM / 8:29 PM

1947: A tarsier from the Philippines arrives at the Bronx Zoo.

9 WEDNESDAY

☼ 5:33 AM / 8:28 PM

1958: Merv Griffin tapes his TV show in Harlem in support of Mayor Lindsay's "Give a Damn" campaign.

10 THURSDAY

☼ 5:34 AM / 8:28 PM
○ FULL MOON

Summer Evenings in the Garden at the Merchant's House Museum (Thursdays, Jun. and Jul.)

11 FRIDAY

☼ 5:35 AM / 8:27 PM

1957: Ticker-tape parade for Harlem-born Althea Gibson, the first Black American to win at Wimbledon.

12 SATURDAY

☼ 5:35 AM / 8:27 PM

1893: Crowds gather to watch French Balloon Captain Emile Cartron ascend in a balloon from Manhattan Field, 155th St. and Eighth Ave.

13 SUNDAY

☼ 5:36 AM / 8:26 PM

1865: P. T. Barnum's American Museum burns to the ground.

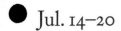 Jul. 14–20

"To be born in the street means to wander all your life, to be free. It means accident and incident, drama, movement."
—Henry Miller

14 MONDAY

☼ 5:37 AM / 8:26 PM

Celebrate Bastille Day at the French Institute Alliance Française.

15 TUESDAY

☼ 5:38 AM / 8:25 PM

1977: New York State's "I Love New York" campaign—developed by advertising pioneer Mary Wells Lawrence with Milton Glaser's unforgettable logo—kicks off.

16 WEDNESDAY

☼ 5:38 AM / 8:25 PM

1927: Dr. Seuss's first cartoon is published in the *Saturday Evening Post*—the $25 sale encourages him to move to NYC.

17 THURSDAY

☼ 5:39 AM / 8:24 PM   ☽ 3RD QUARTER

1976: Seven farmers show up at Union Square for the city's first Greenmarket.

18 FRIDAY

☼ 5:40 AM / 8:23 PM

1936: "Lucky" Luciano is sentenced to 30–50 years in Sing Sing.

19 SATURDAY

☼ 5:41 AM / 8:23 PM

1947: The Greater New York CIO Council holds a straw poll to demonstrate against the NYC Transit Commission's proposed fare hike.

20 SUNDAY

☼ 5:42 AM / 8:22 PM

Last chance to see *Changing the Face of Democracy: Shirley Chisholm at 100* at the Museum of the City of New York

Jul. 21–27

"New York lay stretched in mid-summer languor under her trees in her thinnest dress, idly and beautifully."
 —E. B. White

21 MONDAY

☼ 5:43 AM / 8:21 PM

1971: The *New York Times* reports on TAKI 183, a Manhattan teenager who popularized tagging with his name and street—though he said he "took the form from JULIO 204."

22 TUESDAY

☼ 5:43 AM / 8:20 PM ♌ LEO

1871: The *New York Times* publishes "The Secret Accounts"—an exposé of extravagant spending and kick-backs on construction of the Tweed Courthouse, leading to William "Boss" Tweed's indictment.

23 WEDNESDAY

☼ 5:44 AM / 8:19 PM

1788: Five thousand New Yorkers march in a parade in support of New York's ratification of the U.S. Constitution.

24 THURSDAY

☼ 5:45 AM / 8:18 PM
● NEW MOON

1952: Count Basie opens with a new orchestra at Birdland on West 52nd St.

25 FRIDAY

☼ 5:46 AM / 8:18 PM

1822: Cornerstone is laid for Saint James Cathedral, the oldest Catholic church in Brooklyn.

26 SATURDAY

☼ 5:47 AM / 8:17 PM

1903: Horatio Nelson Jackson and Sewall Crocker—the first men to drive across the U.S.—arrive in NYC from San Francisco, 63 days, 12 hours, and 30 minutes later.

27 SUNDAY

☼ 5:48 AM / 8:16 PM

1972: Jane Fonda lands at JFK from her trip to North Vietnam—and is soon nicknamed "Hanoi Jane."

● Jul. 28–Aug. 3

"New York, the capsized city, half-capsized anyway, with the inhabitants hanging on, most of them still able to laugh as they cling to their island that is their life's predicament."
—Maeve Brennan

28 MONDAY

☼ 5:49 AM / 8:15 PM

1855: Art patron and suffragist Louisine Havemeyer, whose bequest transformed the Metropolitan Museum of Art, is born in New York.

29 TUESDAY

☼ 5:50 AM / 8:14 PM

1957: Floyd Patterson wins by TKO in round ten of fifteen against Tommy "Hurricane" Jackson during the Heavyweight Title Bout at the Polo Grounds.

30 WEDNESDAY

☼ 5:51 AM / 8:13 PM

1981: Robert Moses dies.

31 THURSDAY

☼ 5:52 AM / 8:12 PM

1937: Five thousand WPA workers picket the program's headquarters to protest layoffs and demand support for a bill that would extend work relief.

1 FRIDAY

☼ 5:53 AM / 8:11 PM ◑ 1ST QUARTER

1981: MTV launches with the music video for "Video Killed the Radio Star" by the Buggles.

2 SATURDAY

☼ 5:54 AM / 8:09 PM

1951: Sugar Ray Robinson is given a New York City scroll for distinguished public service at a City Hall ceremony.

3 SUNDAY

☼ 5:55 AM / 8:08 PM

Last chance to see *The Three Perfections: Japanese Poetry, Calligraphy, and Painting from the Mary and Cheney Cowles Collection* at the Met

AUGUST

New York has been called the "mecca" of basketball. No other city boasts three top-tier professional teams (well, besides LA). But the heart of the city game isn't found at the **Garden** or **Barclays Center**. You find it instead on the cracked concrete courts with orange steel rims, usually missing a net, of one of the city's 1,800 outdoor courts—like **Harlem's Rucker Park** where pros like Dr. J and Kevin Durant have faced local legends such as Joe "the Destroyer" Hammond, stars like Kareem Abdul-Jabbar first learned how to play a city-style game, and little girls like Chamique Holdsclaw called "I got next." Summer tournaments can be found at **Dyckman Park in Washington Heights and "The Cage" on West 4th Street**, while any court is open for pickup games. If basketball isn't for you, **Harlem Week**, the **Dominican Day Parade**, and **Summer Streets** are perfect ways to pass a hot August day.

Professor Vaticinate says, *August starts off hot, but relief is just a cold front away by the 7th, followed by a short bucolic frolic. Then, a brief dose of heavy showers and storms, hopefully moving out before the 11th through 13th; then look for meteorites if clear those nights. Midmonth is fair and pleasant, but then, here we go again: more likely hot than not. During this latest heat wave, we're all frequent fryers, so keep a beach within reach. Here's a palindrome that's perfect for this weather: "Too hot to hoot."*

NORMALS FOR
CENTRAL PARK
Avg. high: 83.3°
Avg. low: 68.9°
Avg. rainfall: 4.56"

On balmy summer evenings, if you ever wonder what the temperature might be but lack a thermometer, just listen for the sound of the chirp of a cricket. The frequency of chirping varies according to temperature. To get a rough estimate of the temperature in degrees Fahrenheit, count the number of chirps in fifteen seconds and then add thirty-seven. The number you get will be a good approximation of the outside temperature.

Sky Watch: The Perseid meteors are one of our most active and reliable meteor showers and will peak during the predawn hours of the 12th, but this year the number of meteors will be substantially reduced by the bright light of the Moon. As a consolation prize, that very same morning, look low to the east-northeast after 4 a.m. for an eye-catching pairing of the two brightest planets, Venus and Jupiter.

ANNALS OF THE NIGHT SKY

Believe it or not, the Moon is half as bright as a full Moon for only about 2.4 days before and after full phase. Even though about 95 percent of the Moon is illuminated at this time, and to most casual observers it might still look like a "full" Moon, its brightness is roughly 0.7 magnitudes less than when it's full, making it appear one-half as bright.

NYC BOOK OF THE MONTH
Zami: A New Spelling of My Name
by Audre Lorde (1982)

Lorde's "biomythography" paints an evocative picture of her Harlem upbringing, remembering "the smell of the filled Harlem streets during summer, after a brief shower or the spraying drizzle of the watering trucks released the rank smell of the pavements to the sun," and "stopping to search for hidden pennies winking like kittens under the subway gratings."

NYC MOVIE OF THE MONTH
Kids, directed by Larry Clark, starring Leo Fitzpatrick,
Justin Pierce, and Chloë Sevigny (1995)

Writer Harmony Korine was inspired by the city's skateboard culture, where he cast many of the film's actors—all untrained, including soon-to-be "it" girl Chloë Sevigny. It was filmed with such naturalism that Janet Maslin in the *Times* suggested to think of it "not as cinema verite but as a new strain of post-apocalyptic science fiction, using hyperbole to magnify a kernel of terrible, undeniable truth."

August has 31 days.

Aug. 4–10

"Not only is New York City the nation's melting pot. It is also the casserole, the chafing dish, and the charcoal grill."
—John Lindsay

4 MONDAY

☼ 5:55 AM / 8:07 PM

1976: Spider Webb tattoos a woman outside of MoMA to protest a 1966 law forbidding the practice.

5 TUESDAY

☼ 5:56 AM / 8:06 PM

1964: Future Beastie Boy Adam Yauch is born in Brooklyn.

6 WEDNESDAY

☼ 5:57 AM / 8:05 PM

International Puppet Fringe Festival of New York (IPFFNYC), produced by Teatro SEA in partnership with The Clemente (through Aug. 13).

7 THURSDAY

●

☼ 5:58 AM / 8:04 PM

1986: Spike Lee's *She's Gotta Have It* opens in theaters.

8 FRIDAY

☼ 5:59 AM / 8:02 PM

1885: Ulysses S. Grant is laid to rest in a temporary tomb in Riverside Park.

9 SATURDAY

☼ 6:00 AM / 8:01 PM   ○ FULL MOON

1997: Abner Louima is brutally beaten by police.

10 SUNDAY

☼ 6:01 AM / 8:00 PM

Dominican Day Parade, Sixth Ave.

 Aug. 11–17

"Being on that layup line at Mount Morris, listening to 'Body Rock,' wearing a Holcombe Rucker tournament shirt—that's where the crossroads of rock, rubber, 45s came together."
—Bobbito Garcia

11 MONDAY

☼ 6:02 AM / 7:58 PM

1970: McSorley's Old Ale House admits women for the first time.

12 TUESDAY

☼ 6:03 AM / 7:57 PM

1981: IBM unveils its first personal computer at the Waldorf Astoria.

13 WEDNESDAY

☼ 6:04 AM / 7:56 PM

2007: Philanthropist Brooke Astor dies.

14 THURSDAY

☼ 6:05 AM / 7:54 PM

1944: Weegee photographs the aftermath of a fire at Coney Island's Luna Park.

15 FRIDAY

☼ 6:06 AM / 7:53 PM

1858: The cornerstone of Saint Patrick's Cathedral is laid.

16 SATURDAY

☼ 6:07 AM / 7:52 PM   ◑ 3RD QUARTER

Feast of Saint Rocco

1946: City College hosts a benefit concert with Duke Ellington and Billie Holiday for Isaac Woodard, an African American sergeant brutally beaten by white police officers.

17 SUNDAY

☼ 6:08 AM / 7:50 PM

1948: Babe Ruth's funeral is held at Yankee Stadium.

Aug. 18–24

"The phrase 'I got next' is synonymous with streetball culture. It's a rallying cry to say, 'I'm ready for war.'"
   —Priscilla Edwards

18 MONDAY

☼ 6:09 AM / 7:49 PM

1982: For the first time, one hundred million shares are traded in a single day on the New York Stock Exchange.

19 TUESDAY

☼ 6:10 AM / 7:47 PM

1930: Six thousand people line up outside an unemployment office on Lafayette St.—135 get jobs.

20 WEDNESDAY

☼ 6:11 AM / 7:46 PM

1945: Dozens of recently laid-off wartime workers seek peacetime jobs at the NYC office of the War Manpower Commission's Employment Service on Madison Ave.

21 THURSDAY

☼ 6:12 AM / 7:44 PM

1978: Dolly Parton surprises fans with a lunchtime concert on the steps of City Hall the day before her sold-out performance at the Palladium.

22 FRIDAY

☼ 6:13 AM / 7:43 PM ♍ VIRGO

1823: A yellow fever outbreak starts in Brooklyn.

23 SATURDAY

☼ 6:14 AM / 7:41 PM ● NEW MOON

1926: Silent-film star Rudolph Valentino dies in New York.

24 SUNDAY

☼ 6:15 AM / 7:40 PM

1775: A cannonball crashes through the roof of Fraunces Tavern after patriots attempt to seize cannons from British troops at the Battery.

● Aug. 25–31

"What makes New York the mecca of basketball? Is it New York's legendary playgrounds? The world famous arenas? The hype? . . . it's about winning. Winning is key in New York City."
—Walt "Clyde" Frazier

25 MONDAY

☼ 6:16 AM / 7:38 PM

U.S. Open Tennis tournament begins at the Billie Jean King National Tennis Center in Flushing, Queens.

26 TUESDAY

☼ 6:17 AM / 7:37 PM

1949: Gayle McKinney-Griffith, a founder and star of Dance Theatre of Harlem, is born in Harlem.

27 WEDNESDAY

☼ 6:18 AM / 7:35 PM

2004: Five thousand cyclists show up for a Critical Mass ride during the Republican National Convention; police make mass arrests at the ride's end point in the East Village.

28 THURSDAY

☼ 6:19 AM / 7:34 PM

1965: Bob Dylan plays Forest Hills Tennis Stadium—the first show after his controversial appearance with electric guitar at the Newport Folk Festival.

29 FRIDAY

☼ 6:20 AM / 7:32 PM

1921: Iris Apfel is born in Astoria, Queens.

30 SATURDAY

☼ 6:21 AM / 7:30 PM

Richmond County Fair at Historic Richmond Town, Staten Island (through Sep. 1)

31 SUNDAY

☼ 6:22 AM / 7:29 PM   ◑ 1ST QUARTER

1919: A city police boat ferries hundreds to Brooklyn and Coney Island during a Brooklyn Rapid Transit streetcar strike.

SEPTEMBER

TODAY THEY SEEM LIKE steadfast fixtures of the urban land-scape found year-round every day of the week in every borough, but when the city's greenmarkets first opened in 1976, founder Barry Benepe remembers, "the drug dealers would tell the farmers that it wasn't safe to come [to Union Square]." Today the **Union Square Greenmarket** is just as likely to be visited by celebrity chefs and foodies as it is by editors from the *New York Times* style section hunting for fresh looks instead of fresh greens. September is not too late to pick up some late summer bounty —sunflowers, pumpkins, and apples—at the city's numerous **greenmarkets,** just be sure to dress for the occasion.

PROFESSOR VATICINATE SAYS, *heat ends with a bang on Labor Day (thunderstorms), followed by seven wondrous days, we say. From the 8th to 11th, we might need to watch offshore for a possible hurricane. That's also when supermarkets fill with people who don't want to be caught with their pantries down. Thereafter, cloudiness will lift, followed by unfailing clear sailing through the start of autumn. It's too cool for the pool, though. Heavy showers and thunderstorms finish out the month.*

NORMALS FOR
CENTRAL PARK

Avg. high: 76.2°
Avg. low: 62.3°
Avg. rainfall: 4.31"

September 27 marks the fortieth anniversary of Hurricane Gloria, which brought damaging winds throughout southeast New York. At Central Park, winds up to 51 mph were reported, but across central and eastern Long Island there were reports of gusts of 85 to possibly 115 mph. At Battery Park a storm surge reached nearly seven feet high, and about 1.5 million people in New York State lost power.

SKY WATCH: On the 19th, at around 5:15 a.m., look low near the east-northeast horizon to see a lovely waning crescent Moon; just below it will be dazzling Venus, and just below Venus will be the bluish star Regulus. Venus outshines the star by a ratio of 120 to 1. The bright star visible overhead at around 9 p.m. on the 22nd is Deneb in Cygnus the Swan, which points southwest these evenings, as if migrating from the onset of cold weather.

ANNALS OF THE NIGHT SKY

Back in 1970, the watch company Helbros asked Dr. Kenneth L. Franklin, the chief scientist at the Hayden Planetarium, to design a watch for astronauts to use on the Moon. Interestingly, one Moon watch was sent to the president of the United States at that time, Richard M. Nixon, who sent a thank-you note to Franklin. The note and another Moon watch were kept in a display case at the Hayden Planetarium for several years.

NYC BOOK OF THE MONTH
Olga Dies Dreaming by Xochitl Gonzalez (2022)

Sister and brother—Olga, a wedding planner, and Pedro, a politician—attempt to build a life radically different from their radical parents, one-time members of the Young Lords (Puerto Rican New Yorkers' answer to the Black Panthers). The plot deepens as Hurricane Maria devastates Puerto Rico, where their mother went after she abandoned them to live with their grandmother in Brooklyn, long ago.

NYC MOVIE OF THE MONTH
The Squid and the Whale, directed by Noah Baumbach, starring Jeff Daniels, Laura Linney, and Owen Kline (2005)

This film about the dissolution of a marriage, set in the 1980s in bookish Park Slope, takes its title from an underwater diorama at the American Museum of Natural History—a metaphor for what it means to feel both scared and safe. Baumbach filmed it in the brownstone of a childhood friend and dressed Daniels in his own father's clothes.

September has 30 days.

Sep. 1–7

"The markets take on the festive air of a street fair ... exclaiming at the crackling evergreen sparkle of spinach or the ruffled silkiness of spring green leaf lettuce."
　　—Mimi Sheraton,
　　　New York Times, 1977

1　MONDAY

☿ 6:23 AM / 7:27 PM

Labor Day

West Indian Carnival (and J'ouvert) in Crown Heights, Brooklyn

2　TUESDAY

☿ 6:24 AM / 7:26 PM

1930: French pilots Dieudonné Costes and Maurice Bellonte are given a ticker-tape parade after completing the first nonstop flight from Paris to New York.

3　WEDNESDAY

☿ 6:25 AM / 7:24 PM

1821: A hurricane makes landfall in Jamaica Bay, causing a thirteen-foot storm surge and flooding south of Canal St.

4　THURSDAY　●

☿ 6:26 AM / 7:22 PM

1964: The Animals perform their first U.S. concert at the Paramount Theater.

5　FRIDAY

☿ 6:27 AM / 7:21 PM

The International Center of Photography hosts the ICP Photobook Fest, welcoming photobook publishers from around the world (through Sep. 7).

6　SATURDAY

☿ 6:28 AM / 7:19 PM

1776: A one-man submarine called the *Turtle* attempts to sink the sixty-four-gun British flagship *Eagle*.

7　SUNDAY

☿ 6:29 AM / 7:17 PM　○ FULL MOON

1995: Calvin Klein opens his flagship store on the northeast corner of Madison Ave. and 60th St.

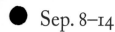 Sep. 8–14

"The history of New York is as fine and flamboyant a tale as your six favorite novelists could write in collaboration."
—*New Yorker*, 1927

8 MONDAY

☼ 6:30 AM / 7:16 PM

1880: The Manhattan Market at 34th St. and Eleventh Ave.—a competitor of Tammany-backed Washington Market—is destroyed in a suspicious fire.

9 TUESDAY

☼ 6:31 AM / 7:14 PM

1966: Performance artist Charlotte Moorman enacts "Morning Glory" by Wolf Vostell—putting perfumed pages of the *New York Times* into a blender during the Avant Garde Art Festival.

10 WEDNESDAY

☼ 6:32 AM / 7:12 PM

1990: Ellis Island reopens to the public after a $156 million restoration.

11 THURSDAY

☼ 6:33 AM / 7:11 PM

Commemorations of the World Trade Center attack at the 9/11 Memorial

12 FRIDAY

☼ 6:34 AM / 7:09 PM

1954: Marilyn Monroe and Joe DiMaggio are photographed dining at El Morocco.

13 SATURDAY

☼ 6:35 AM / 7:07 PM

1929: Communist mayoral candidate William Weinstone speaks to a crowd of supporters at 130th St. and Lenox Ave.

14 SUNDAY

☼ 6:36 AM / 7:06 PM ◑ 3RD QUARTER

2015: Adam Purple, who in 1975 began creating a garden that would extend fifteen thousand square feet in abandoned Lower East Side lots, dies.

Sep. 15–21

"Whenever I return to the city, I expect to be filled with nostalgic wonder. But the minute I step into the subway I'm immediately filled with an old familiar rage."
    —Julia Wertz

---

15 MONDAY
☼ 6:37 AM / 7:04 PM

2011: Steuben Glass closes their flagship Manhattan store after seventy-seven years.

---

16 TUESDAY
☼ 6:38 AM / 7:02 PM

1920: A Wall Street bombing, still unresolved.

---

17 WEDNESDAY
☼ 6:38 AM / 7:01 PM

1986: Ivan Boesky, who told business school graduates "greed is all right, by the way," turns himself in to federal authorities on insider trading charges.

18 THURSDAY ●
☼ 6:39 AM / 6:59 PM

1851: First issue of the *New York Daily Times* (now the *New York Times*) is published.

---

19 FRIDAY
☼ 6:40 AM / 6:57 PM

Feast of San Gennaro

1930: Governor Al Smith lays the cornerstone of the Empire State Building.

---

20 SATURDAY
☼ 6:41 AM / 6:56 PM

German American Steuben Parade, Fifth Ave.

---

21 SUNDAY
☼ 6:42 AM / 6:54 PM ● NEW MOON

1846: A. T. Stewart's Marble Palace, the first American department store, opens. It still stands at Broadway and Reade Sts.

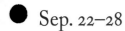# Sep. 22–28

"Taking cabs in the middle of
the night
driving as if to save your soul where
the road goes round and round
the park
and the meter glares like a moral owl"
—Elizabeth Bishop

22 MONDAY

☼ 6:43 AM / 6:52 PM ♎ LIBRA

Autumnal Equinox
Rosh Hashanah begins.

1962: Pete Seeger headlines (and Bob
Dylan performs at) a *Hootenanny at
Carnegie Hall.*

23 TUESDAY

☼ 6:44 AM / 6:50 PM

1923: Kahlil Gibran's *The Prophet* is
published by Alfred A. Knopf.

24 WEDNESDAY

☼ 6:45 AM / 6:49 PM

Rosh Hashanah ends.

1957: Only 6,702 people attend the
Brooklyn Dodgers' final game, a win
against the Pittsburg Pirates, at
Ebbets Field.

25 THURSDAY

☼ 6:46 AM / 6:47 PM

1909: The Hudson-Fulton Celebration
commemorates the 300th anniversary
of Henry Hudson's discovery of the
Hudson River and the 100th anniversary of Robert Fulton's paddle steamer.

26 FRIDAY

☼ 6:47 AM / 6:45 PM

1898: George Gershwin is born at
242 Snediker Ave., Brooklyn.

27 SATURDAY

☼ 6:48 AM / 6:44 PM

The Clemente Open Studios, with
more than fifty studio artists and
organizations opening their doors
(and 28th)

28 SUNDAY

☼ 6:49 AM / 6:42 PM

1891: Herman Melville dies in
obscurity at 104 East 26th St.

Sep. 29–Oct. 5

"We sighed as we set foot on solid ground. There, gaping before us, were the jaws of the iron dragon: the immense New York metropolis."
—Bernardo Vega, 1955

---

29 MONDAY

☼ 6:50 AM / 6:40 PM ◑ IST QUARTER

1957: New York Giants baseball team play their final game, a loss to the Pittsburg Pirates, at the Polo Grounds.

---

30 TUESDAY

☼ 6:51 AM / 6:39 PM

1899: Theodore Roosevelt rides horseback in a parade for Admiral George Dewey, following the admiral's victory at the Battle of Manila Bay that ended the Spanish-American War.

I WEDNESDAY

☼ 6:52 AM / 6:37 PM

1971: At the first NYC Marathon in which women were allowed to participate, six women sit at the starting line for ten minutes to protest a mandated separate start time for their sex.

---

2 THURSDAY

☼ 6:53 AM / 6:35 PM ●

Yom Kippur

1973: Martin Scorsese's *Mean Streets* premieres at the New York Film Festival.

---

3 FRIDAY

☼ 6:54 AM / 6:34 PM

1951: New York Giants' Bobby Thompson hits a three-run homer off the Dodgers' Ralph Branca to win the National League Pennant—baseball's "Shot Heard 'Round the World."

---

4 SATURDAY

☼ 6:55 AM / 6:32 PM

Pumpkin picking at Historic Richmond Town's Decker Farm (Sat. and Sun. through Oct.)

---

5 SUNDAY

☼ 6:57 AM / 6:31 PM

Last chance to see *You Are Here: An Immersive Film Experience* at the Museum of the City of New York

OCTOBER

NEW YORKERS LOVE DOGS. If you don't believe it, remember the uproar when the **Tompkins Square Park Halloween Dog Parade** was almost canceled in 2023. That parade, along with **Fort Greene's Great PUPkin Dog Costume Contest,** gives pups—or rather, their owners—a chance to let loose their creativity. The best costumes touch on urban issues—like 2022's dog/lanternfly and owner/shoe duo, or that dog dressed as a bodega cat. Of course, there are other reasons to love October—like **Open House New York,** special **Oktoberfest brews from Brooklyn Brewery or the Bronx's Gun Hill Brewing,** and **Pumpkin Nights at the Bronx Zoo.**

PROFESSOR VATICINATE SAYS, *fair to start the month, then a change to rain. Over the high-terrain regions north and west of NYC, some wet flakes might even mix in. Living up to its reputation for clear skies, a ten-day spell of fair/dry weather beginning on the 8th; great for leaf-peeping. Then, during October's final week, praise the rain that strips the trees, and carpets the land with leaves. Hoping for fine weather for Halloween? That might be "squishful thinking."*

NORMALS FOR
CENTRAL PARK
Avg. high: 64.5°
Avg. low: 51.4°
Avg. rainfall: 4.38"
Avg. snowfall: 0.1"

October is recognized as the clearest month, with almost 39 percent of its days cloud-free or nearly so. But October can also be a month of extremes. The latest date in the year that the temperature has hit 90° came on October 17, 1938. The earliest snowfall of 1" or more was on October 29, 2011 (2.9"). The greatest one-day amount of rain (11.17") occurred on October 8–9, 1903. Conversely, the longest stretch of days (thirty-six) in which no measurable precipitation fell began on October 9, 1924.

October is the clearest month: 12 days average less than 3/10 cloud cover.

SKY WATCH: Check out the nearly full Moon after sundown on the 5th and you'll see Saturn shining below it. The next night is the harvest Moon. Around 1 a.m. on the 14th, you can watch the Moon ascend the east-northeast sky, accompanied by brilliant Jupiter off to its right. Finally, at around 6:30 a.m. on the 19th, look low near the east-southeast horizon to sight Venus sitting to the left of a slender crescent Moon.

ANNALS OF THE NIGHT SKY

The 2nd will mark the ninetieth anniversary of the opening of the Hayden Planetarium. On that night in 1935, a cosmic ray from interstellar space was trapped by a delicate electrical apparatus and provided the impulse that switched on the great planetarium projector for eight hundred invited guests.

NYC BOOK OF THE MONTH
The Amazing Adventures of Kavalier & Clay
by Michael Chabon (2000)

Chabon's fable of escape, magic, and comic books begins, as his Brooklyn-born character Sam Clay recalls, "in 1939, toward the end of October," when his mysterious cousin Josef Kavalier appears in his doorway after escaping Nazi persecution. Inspired by real-life comic book creators like Jack Kirby and Stan Lee, Chabon spent a month wandering Manhattan for "street and building research."

NYC MOVIE OF THE MONTH
Hair, directed by Miloš Forman, starring John Savage,
Treat Williams, and Beverly D'Angelo (1979)

This movie adaptation of the groundbreaking 1967 musical was filmed in October 1977 at Central Park landmarks including Bethesda Fountain, Sheep Meadow, and the bridle path. Although producers of the stage show felt the film turned their "tribe" of hippies into "oddballs," the film recalls the real-life moment in the late 1960s when Central Park hosted several "be-ins" to protest the Vietnam War.

October has 31 days.

 Oct. 6–12

"Autumn thunderstorms, leaf fires, the primaeval stillness that comes after a heavy snowfall and the randy smells of April all seem magnified by the pavings of the greatest city in the world."
—John Cheever

6 MONDAY

☼ 6:58 AM / 6:29 PM ○ FULL MOON

Sukkot begins.

1982: *Everybody*, Madonna's debut single, is released by Sire Records.

7 TUESDAY

☼ 6:59 AM / 6:27 PM

1913: Rube Marquard throws the first pitch of Game 1 of the World Series for the Giants.

8 WEDNESDAY

☼ 7:00 AM / 6:26 PM

1956: Don Larsen pitches a perfect game for the Yankees in Game 5 of the World Series against the Brooklyn Dodgers.

9 THURSDAY

☼ 7:01 AM / 6:24 PM

1871: Cornelius Vanderbilt's Grand Central Depot (later replaced by Grand Central Terminal) opens.

10 FRIDAY

☼ 7:02 AM / 6:23 PM

1935: Gershwin's *Porgy and Bess* opens at the Alvin Theatre.

11 SATURDAY

☼ 7:03 AM / 6:21 PM

1925: The New York Giants play their first game in the NFL.

12 SUNDAY

☼ 7:04 AM / 6:19 PM

1971: Opening party for *Jesus Christ Superstar* is held at Tavern On the Green.

Oct. 13–19

"He acquired that charming inso-
lence, that irritating completeness,
that sophisticated crassness, that
overbalanced poise that make the
Manhattan gentleman so delight-
fully small in his greatness."
  —O. Henry

13 MONDAY
☼ 7:05 AM / 6:18 PM ◑ 3RD QUARTER

Columbus Day
Indigenous Peoples' Day
Sukkot ends.

Columbus Day Parade on Fifth Ave.
and Indigenous Peoples' Day celebrations at the National Museum of the
American Indian

14 TUESDAY
☼ 7:06 AM / 6:16 PM

1965: The 1832 Old Merchant's House
(now a museum) is the first Manhattan
building designated under the city's
new Landmarks Preservation Law.

15 WEDNESDAY
☼ 7:07 AM / 6:15 PM

1964: An estimated one million Brook-
lynites come to see Lyndon B. Johnson
and Robert Kennedy as they campaign
for president and senate, respectively.

16 THURSDAY
☼ 7:08 AM / 6:13 PM

1888: Eugene O'Neill is born in
New York.

17 FRIDAY
☼ 7:09 AM / 6:12 PM

Open House New York Weekend
(through Oct. 19)

18 SATURDAY
☼ 7:10 AM / 6:10 PM

1980: The Brooklyn Museum opens
Judy Chicago: The Dinner Party—its
New York debut.

19 SUNDAY
☼ 7:11 AM / 6:09 PM

1960: Ticker-tape parade for John F.
Kennedy, who was campaigning in
the city.

 Oct. 20–26

"When you leave New York, you are astonished at how clean the rest of the world is. Clean is not enough."
—Fran Lebowitz

20 MONDAY

☼ 7:13 AM / 6:07 PM

Diwali/Deepavali

1917: Four thousand Boy Scouts take part in a Liberty Loan parade on Fifth Ave. to raise funds for WWI.

21 TUESDAY

☼ 7:14 AM / 6:06 PM ● NEW MOON

1931: Broadway goes dark for one minute to honor Thomas Edison who had died on Oct. 18).

22 WEDNESDAY

☼ 7:15 AM / 6:05 PM ♏ SCORPIO

1939: The Brooklyn Dodgers and Philadelphia Eagles play the first televised professional football game, at Ebbets Field.

23 THURSDAY

☼ 7:16 AM / 6:03 PM

1978: Nora Ephron, George Plimpton, and others publish *Not the New York Times*, spoofing the paper during a writers' strike.

24 FRIDAY

☼ 7:17 AM / 6:02 PM

Candlelight Ghost Tours of Merchant's House Museum: "Manhattan's Most Haunted House" (and Oct. 25, 30)

25 SATURDAY

☼ 7:18 AM / 6:00 PM

1977: Thirty activists demanding independence for Puerto Rico occupy the Statue of Liberty, draping a Puerto Rican flag from its crown.

26 SUNDAY

☼ 7:19 AM / 5:59 PM

Halloween on the Farm at Queens County Farm

Oct. 27–Nov. 2

"What is barely hinted at in other American cities is condensed and enlarged in New York."
 —Saul Bellow

27 MONDAY
☼ 7:20 AM / 5:58 PM

1904: NYC Subway opens.

28 TUESDAY
☼ 7:22 AM / 5:56 PM

1886: The Statue of Liberty is dedicated with a ticker-tape parade attended by more than one million people, a boat parade of three hundred vessels, and a formal unveiling on Bedloe's Island.

29 WEDNESDAY
☼ 7:23 AM / 5:55 PM   ◐ 1ST QUARTER

Red Hook's Barnacle Parade celebrates the neighborhood's resilience on the anniversary of Hurricane Sandy.

30 THURSDAY
☼ 7:24 AM / 5:54 PM

1958: Washington Square Park is officially closed to automobile traffic.

31 FRIDAY
☼ 7:25 AM / 5:53 PM

Halloween

Greenwich Village Halloween Parade

1 SATURDAY
☼ 7:26 AM / 5:51 PM

BORIMIX Festival celebrating Puerto Rican Heritage Month at The Clemente (through Nov. 30, with public events Nov. 2–9)

2 SUNDAY
☼ 6:27 AM / 4:50 PM

Daylight saving time ends.

New York City Marathon

NOVEMBER

NOVEMBER WRAPS UP with a four-word salute—not the Bronx kind—to the holiday season: "Let's have a parade!" Although it's not the oldest Thanksgiving Day parade in the country (Philadelphia beat it by four years), the **Macy's Parade** is certainly the best known, beamed into TV sets across the nation since 1948. The city's sharp edges get a little softer as eager marching bands, delighted children, and performers from across the country converge on Herald Square. Don't forget to cheer on the **marathon** runners, **peep fall foliage at Brooklyn's Green-Wood Cemetery or Staten Island's Clove Lakes Park,** and visit a **holiday market** for hot apple cider and unique gifts.

PROFESSOR VATICINATE SAYS, *set clocks back on the 2nd, and on the same day, the TCS Marathon is run under ideal conditions: fair and cold. Then cover your keister by the 7th; it's a nor'easter, and . . . are those flakes mixing in? During November's second week, better make a levee: rain's still heavy, and still windy too. Clearing skies for midmonth, then turning unsettled once again. Hopefully it clears by Turkey Day. Give thanks this verse isn't worse!*

NORMALS FOR
CENTRAL PARK
Avg. high: 54.0°
Avg. low: 42.0°
Avg. rainfall: 3.58"
Avg. snowfall: 0.5"

November 25 will mark the seventy-fifth anniversary of a 1950 storm that was then described by the U.S. Weather Bureau as "the most violent of its kind ever recorded in the northeastern quarter of the United States." Along with heavy wind and rain damage along the Atlantic coast, as much as thirty inches of snow fell in Ohio and western Pennsylvania. Five people were killed in NYC, and thirty-three in the suburbs. The financial loss in the Northeastern U.S. exceeded $100 million.

SKY WATCH: The full Moon makes its closest approach to Earth this year (221,726 miles) on the 5th at 5 p.m.—known as a "supermoon." The Moon will pay Saturn a visit twice this month: on the 1st it will be positioned to the upper right of the ringed planet, and on the 29th, you'll see it sitting to its upper left. Cassiopeia's bright letter M is high in the north sky, while the Big Dipper skims low above the north horizon.

ANNALS OF THE NIGHT SKY

Ornithologists and bird-watchers will likely be aiming small telescopes at this month's full Moon to sight the fleeting silhouettes of a wide variety of migrating birds. In fact, "Moon watching" is a term that ornithologists still use to record nocturnally migrating birds. One particularly noteworthy discovery that came out of this practice is the amazing fact that birds will journey nonstop for hundreds of miles across the Gulf of Mexico.

NYC BOOK OF THE MONTH
Delirious New York: A Retroactive Manifesto for Manhattan
by Rem Koolhaas (1978)

Koolhaas argues that Manhattan "is a mountain range of evidence without manifesto" and sets out to divine the island's essence through an artful examination of its peculiar architecture, history, and literature—from early Coney Island's blinding electric lights to the "needle and the globe" of the 1939 World's Fair.

NYC MOVIE OF THE MONTH
42nd Street, directed by Lloyd Bacon, starring Warner Baxter, Bebe Daniels, and George Brent (1933)

This backstage musical was filmed entirely at Warner Bros. Studios in Burbank, but with a racy (pre-Code) plot and hallucinogenic "chorus line" choreography by Busby Berkeley, its soul is all Broadway. It features the memorable line that every ingenue who comes to New York wants to hear: "You're going out a youngster, but you've got to come back a star!"

November has 30 days.

 Nov. 3–9

"People in New York love to tell you how exhausted they are. Then they fall apart when someone says, 'Yeah, you look pretty tired.'"
—David Sedaris

3 MONDAY
☼ 6:29 AM / 4:49 PM

1900: Madison Square Garden holds its first automobile show.

4 TUESDAY
☼ 6:30 AM / 4:48 PM

Election Day

1859: The Great Hall at Cooper Union opens.

5 WEDNESDAY
☼ 6:31 AM / 4:47 PM ○ FULL MOON

1932: Franklin D. Roosevelt makes his last major campaign speech for the presidency at a rally at Madison Square Garden.

6 THURSDAY
☼ 6:32 AM / 4:46 PM

1895: Consuelo Vanderbilt marries the 9th Duke of Marlborough; Byron Co. shoots paparazzi-style photos of the couple leaving Saint Thomas Church.

7 FRIDAY
☼ 6:33 AM / 4:45 PM

1929: MoMA's first exhibition—titled *Cézanne, Gauguin, Seurat, van Gogh*—opens.

8 SATURDAY
☼ 6:34 AM / 4:44 PM

1725: William Bradford publishes the *New York Gazette*, the city's first newspaper.

9 SUNDAY
☼ 6:36 AM / 4:43 PM

1912: Elizabeth Arden hands out red lipstick to marchers advocating for women's right to vote.

Nov. 10–16

"There is little in New York that does not spring from money. It is not a town of ideas; it is not even a town of causes."
    —H. L. Mencken

10 MONDAY

☿ 6:37 AM / 4:42 PM

1969: *Sesame Street* begins broadcasting.

11 TUESDAY

☿ 6:38 AM / 4:41 PM

Veterans Day

1807: Washington Irving nicknames NYC "Gotham" for the first time in his magazine, *Salmagundi*.

12 WEDNESDAY

☿ 6:39 AM / 4:40 PM   ☽ 3RD QUARTER

1945: Crowds gather at a vacant lot between Villa Ave. and Grand Concourse in the Bronx, hoping to see a vision of the Virgin Mary after a boy claimed seeing her image there on Oct. 30.

13 THURSDAY

☿ 6:40 AM / 4:39 PM

1904: Holland Tunnel opens.

14 FRIDAY

☿ 6:42 AM / 4:38 PM

1974: The International Center of Photography opens its doors for the first time, with the mission of championing socially and politically minded images that can educate and change the world.

15 SATURDAY

☿ 6:43 AM / 4:37 PM

1962: Judith Malina of the Living Theatre joins an anti–Vietnam War demonstration near Judson Church in Greenwich Village.

16 SUNDAY

☿ 6:44 AM / 4:36 PM

1801: The first edition of Alexander Hamilton's *New York Evening Post* is published (the city's oldest extant paper).

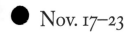 Nov. 17–23

"New York is an arrogant city....
There is no pretense here of ex-
cessive gentility, and the rush was
always to the new, the large, the
prosperous, the fashionable."
—Paul Goldberger

17 MONDAY

☼ 6:45 AM / 4:36 PM

1899: Trolleys begin running on
Broadway.

18 TUESDAY

☼ 6:46 AM / 4:35 PM

1774: Samuel Ellis purchases and builds
a tavern on the island that now bears
his name.

19 WEDNESDAY

☼ 6:47 AM / 4:34 PM

1957: A professional wrestling match
at Madison Square Garden turns into
a riot with five hundred participants,
and ends with three hundred damaged
chairs.

20 THURSDAY

☼ 6:49 AM / 4:34 PM ● NEW MOON

1974: Cher and Bob Mackie, arm in
arm, attend the Metropolitan Museum
of Art's Costume Institute Gala.

21 FRIDAY

☼ 6:50 AM / 4:33 PM ♐ SAGITTARIUS

1924: Leo Hershkowitz, who saved
countless New York City historic
records from the dumpster, is born in
the Bronx.

22 SATURDAY

☼ 6:51 AM / 4:32 PM

1847: The Astor Place Opera House
opens with a performance of Verdi's
Ernani.

23 SUNDAY

☼ 6:52 AM / 4:32 PM

1965: David Gahr photographs Pete
Best, the Beatles' original drummer, in
Central Park.

Nov. 24–30

"Stop trying to hold back the holidays . . . yes, there will be damage to your wallet. But look on the bright side: the window displays are free."
—Simon Doonan

24 MONDAY
☼ 6:53 AM / 4:31 PM

1920: The former home of architect Stanford White is opened as a YWCA club for foreign-born girls and women.

25 TUESDAY
☼ 6:54 AM / 4:31 PM

1967: Frank Stella's first solo show opens at Leo Castelli Gallery.

26 WEDNESDAY
☼ 6:55 AM / 4:30 PM

1922: The first technicolor film, *The Toll of the Sea*, premieres in NYC.

27 THURSDAY
☼ 6:56 AM / 4:30 PM

Thanksgiving Day

Macy's Thanksgiving Day Parade

28 FRIDAY
☼ 6:57 AM / 4:30 PM   ◖ 1ST QUARTER

Native American Heritage Day

1910: Members of the Women's Police Reserve volunteer as crossing guards for schoolchildren.

29 SATURDAY
☼ 6:58 AM / 4:29 PM

1954: The ferryboat *Ellis Island* makes its last run as the island is vacated.

30 SUNDAY
☼ 6:59 AM / 4:29 PM

1932: MoMA opens *American Folk Art: The Art of the Common Man in America*

DECEMBER

IN DECEMBER THE CITY puts on its **holiday best**—on a scale that only New York City can pull off, and it's not to be missed. Midtown buildings are tied up in bows, department store windows become fantastic scenes of delight, a light show dazzles on the facade of **Saks Fifth Avenue**, front yards in **Dyker Heights** erupt in lighted Christmas decorations, neighborhood tree lightings pop up from **East Harlem** to **Sunset Park**, and restaurants like **Rolf's** and **Pete's Tavern** stuff themselves with holiday decor. Even local businesses paint their windows with holiday scenes. It's enough to make you wish it was January so you'd have a whole year to look forward to it.

PROFESSOR VATICINATE SAYS, *a bit of bluster, then a filibuster: the first two weeks of December are unsettled with occasional bouts of rain and wet snow. Midmonth sees a poke or two of Sun and a welcome thaw. Then it turns blustery and raw, as scudding clouds fly, throwing rain in your eye as winter's solstice officially arrives. For Christmastime it turns clear and tingling; hear any jingling? The year finally comes to an end with some rain and wet snow, so "wring out" the old!*

NORMALS FOR
CENTRAL PARK
Avg. high: 44.3°
Avg. low: 33.8°
Avg. rainfall: 4.38"
Avg. snowfall: 4.9"

If you are looking for a great stocking stuffer for someone interested in weather, consider meteorologist Jim Witt's Long Range Weather Calendar. Mr. Witt has formulated a method that relies on historic weather patterns, called analogs, in order to forecast what the weather might be in years or even decades in advance. The calendar is augmented by beautiful photos of the Hudson Valley. All proceeds from the calendar go directly to children's charities and, since 1986, Mr. Witt has raised over $6 million. For more details, go to: https://hfyf.org/calendars/.

Sky Watch: The Geminid meteors are considered the best of the annual meteor displays. This year, the prime time to look will be during the overnight hours of the 13th and 14th. On the 17th at around 6:30 a.m., look low in the southeast for a very thin crescent Moon. If you find it, look well to the Moon's left to glimpse the elusive planet Mercury. Southeast in the evening sky is the most spectacular constellation, Orion, with Taurus the Bull to his upper right.

ANNALS OF THE NIGHT SKY

Sixty years ago, on December 15, 1965, Gemini 6A was launched. Flown by astronauts Wally Schirra and Tom Stafford, Gemini 6A rendezvoused with another crewed space capsule, Gemini 7; it marked a space first. Schirra brought a little Christmas spirit to space during the mission, when he claimed to have spotted Santa Claus in orbit, and also became the first human to play a musical instrument in space when he performed "Jingle Bells" on his harmonica.

NYC BOOK OF THE MONTH
Sex and the Single Girl by Helen Gurley Brown (1962)

The sophisticated, stylish, devil-may-care single girl conjured into being by *Cosmopolitan*'s soon-to-be longtime editor Helen Gurley Brown shares a kinship with the city's Carrie Bradshaws. Although not exactly a New York book, it describes a midcentury, big city ethos of glamorous nights out, stylish apartments (on a budget), and casual sexual harassment—and heavily influenced Matthew Weiner's *Mad Men*.

NYC MOVIE OF THE MONTH
Miracle on 34th Street, directed by George Seaton, starring Edmund Gwenn, Maureen O'Hara, and John Payne (1947)

We already know the film's answer to the question it poses: can a department store Santa actually be the *real* Santa? When *Miracle on 34th Street* came out, the *Times* suggested "from now on we shall have more and more movies named after New York's numbered streets . . . *Love on Fifty-third Street* or *Despair on Third Avenue*." All of which sounds plausible.

December has 31 days.

 Dec. 1–7

"Gradually we fitted our disruptive personalities into the contemporary scene of New York. Or rather New York forgot us and let us stay."
—F. Scott Fitzgerald

1 MONDAY

☼ 7:00 AM / 4:29 PM

1957: Buddy Holly performs on Ed Sullivan's *Toast of the Town* variety show.

2 TUESDAY

☼ 7:01 AM / 4:29 PM

"A Christmas Carol" at the Merchant's House: Charles Dickens in New York, 1867 (through Dec. 24)

3 WEDNESDAY

☼ 7:02 AM / 4:28 PM

Rockefeller Center Christmas Tree Lighting

4 THURSDAY

☼ 7:03 AM / 4:28 PM ○ FULL MOON

1783: George Washington gathers officers from the Continental Army to Fraunces Tavern to bid them farewell.

5 FRIDAY

☼ 7:04 AM / 4:28 PM

1876: The Brooklyn Theatre fire kills at least 278 people and eventually leads to changes in theater building codes.

6 SATURDAY

☼ 7:05 AM / 4:28 PM

1933: Judge John Woolsey rules in favor of Random House's right to publish James Joyce's *Ulysses*.

7 SUNDAY

☼ 7:06 AM / 4:28 PM

Pearl Harbor Remembrance Day

1884: The Ottendorfer Library, the city's first free public library, opens.

Dec. 8–14

"Progress is working the devil with us, and we ought to have a place to put the nicest of our things before they are washed out to sea, together with the cracker jack boxes and the orange peels."
—*New Yorker*, 1926

8 MONDAY

☼ 7:07 AM / 4:28 PM

1891: NYC tattoo artist Samuel O'Reilly files the first mechanical patent for a tattoo machine, based on Edison's autographic printing pen.

9 TUESDAY

☼ 7:08 AM / 4:28 PM

1953: Milton Berle marries Ruth Cosgrove in New York.

10 WEDNESDAY

☼ 7:09 AM / 4:28 PM

1946: Journalist and short story writer Damon Runyon dies; his ashes are scattered over Broadway from an airplane.

11 THURSDAY

☼ 7:10 AM / 4:28 PM
◑ 3RD QUARTER

1981: Max's Kansas City closes with performances by Bad Brains and the Beastie Boys.

12 FRIDAY

☼ 7:10 AM / 4:28 PM

1910: Twenty-five-year-old perfume heiress Dorothy Arnold disappears, resulting in New York's oldest cold case.

13 SATURDAY

☼ 7:11 AM / 4:29 PM

2002: *Maid in Manhattan* with Jennifer Lopez, filmed at the Waldorf Astoria, is released.

14 SUNDAY

☼ 7:12 AM / 4:29 PM

Hanukkah begins.

1894: Barney Pressman, founder of Barneys department store, is born in the Lower East Side.

 Dec. 15–21

"How funny you are today
   New York
like Ginger Rogers in *Swingtime*"
   —Frank O'Hara

15 MONDAY

☼ 7:13 AM / 4:29 PM

1963: *Toys by Artists* opens at Betty Parsons Gallery—allowing adult visitors only if accompanied by a child.

16 TUESDAY

☼ 7:13 AM / 4:29 PM

1899: The Brooklyn Children's Museum opens.

17 WEDNESDAY

☼ 7:14 AM / 4:30 PM

1831: Developer Samuel Ruggles creates Gramercy Park.

18 THURSDAY

☼ 7:15 AM / 4:30 PM

1981: Red Grooms' installation piece *Ruckus Manhattan Revival* is presented by Creative Time.

19 FRIDAY

☼ 7:15 AM / 4:31 PM ● NEW MOON

1903: The Williamsburg Bridge opens.

20 SATURDAY

☼ 7:16 AM / 4:31 PM

1981: *Dreamgirls* opens on Broadway.

21 SUNDAY

☼ 7:16 AM / 4:31 PM ♑ CAPRICORN

Winter Solstice

The annual Clement Clarke Moore Memorial Candlelight Service at Church of the Intercession, where the author is buried.

Dec. 22–28

"They've got cars as big as bars
   They've got rivers of gold
But the wind goes right
   through you
It's no place for the old"
   —The Pogues

22 MONDAY

☼ 7:17 AM / 4:32 PM

Hanukkah ends.

1931: Prohibition agents close the original location of Sherman Billingsley's Stork Club at 132 West 58th St.

23 TUESDAY

☼ 7:17 AM / 4:33 PM

1946: A record 8,872,244 people ride the subway in one day.

24 WEDNESDAY

☼ 7:18 AM / 4:33 PM

Christmas Eve

Holiday Lights at the Bronx Zoo

25 THURSDAY

☼ 7:18 AM / 4:34 PM

Christmas Day

Eat at a Chinese restaurant.

26 FRIDAY

☼ 7:18 AM / 4:34 PM

Kwanzaa begins.

1940: *My Sister Eileen* opens at the Biltmore Theater; it runs for 865 performances.

27 SATURDAY

☼ 7:19 AM / 4:35 PM ◐ 1ST QUARTER

1867: Mark Twain is introduced to his future wife, Olivia Langdon, at the Saint Nicholas Hotel.

28 SUNDAY

☼ 7:19 AM / 4:36 PM

1971: Fifteen veterans end their day-and-a-half-long occupation of the Statue of Liberty, protesting the Vietnam War.

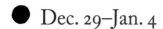 Dec. 29–Jan. 4

"One day the city we built will be gone, and when it goes, we go."
—Colson Whitehead

29 MONDAY

☼ 7:19 AM / 4:37 PM

1934: The first college basketball games at Madison Square Garden are attended by 16,188 fans—Westminster College beats Saint John's and NYU defeats Notre Dame.

30 TUESDAY

☼ 7:19 AM / 4:37 PM

1942: Frank Sinatra makes his solo debut at the Paramount Theater.

31 WEDNESDAY

☼ 7:19 AM / 4:38 PM

New Year's Eve

New York Road Runners Midnight Run in Central Park

1 THURSDAY

☼ 7:20 AM / 4:39 PM

New Year's Day
Kwanzaa ends.

1898: Consolidation of Greater New York creates the five-borough city.

2 FRIDAY

☼ 7:20 AM / 4:40 PM

1946: Demonstrators protest Spanish dictator Francisco Franco outside the Hotel Pennsylvania.

3 SATURDAY

☼ 7:20 AM / 4:41 PM ○ FULL MOON

1857: The first issue of *Harper's Weekly, A Journal of Civilization* is published.

4 SUNDAY

☼ 7:20 AM / 4:42 PM

1982: The Gay Men's Health Crisis, Inc. is formed in New York by Larry Kramer and others.

Contributors

GENERAL EDITOR **Susan Gail Johnson** is a museum consultant, editor, and content developer with a special expertise in New York City. She managed numerous major exhibitions and publications for the Museum of the City of New York and served as project director of its institution-defining permanent exhibition, *New York at Its Core*. Johnson holds a master's degree from NYU's John W. Draper Interdisciplinary Program in Humanities and Social Thought.

ASTRONOMER **Joe Rao** is an Associate and Guest Lecturer at the Hayden Planetarium of the American Museum of Natural History, astronomy columnist for *Natural History* magazine, Night Sky columnist for Space.com, and a contributing editor at *Sky and Telescope* magazine.

METEOROLOGIST **Professor Vaticinate** is the nom de plume of an experienced professional meteorologist.

FASHION FORECASTER **Raissa Bretaña** is a New York–based fashion historian and adjunct instructor at the Fashion Institute of Technology. She also hosts a popular video series for *Glamour*.

ILLUSTRATOR **Andrey Kokorin's** work has appeared in magazines, advertisements, and product packaging around the world.

Compilation copyright © 2024 Abbeville Press. All rights reserved under international copyright conventions. No part of this book may be reproduced or utilized in any form or by any means, electronic or mechanical, including photocopying, recording, or by any information retrieval system, without permission in writing from the publisher. Inquiries should be addressed to Abbeville Press, 655 Third Avenue, New York, NY 10017. The text of this book was set in Caslon Pro. Printed in Türkiye.

ISBN 978-0-7892-5471-9

Fourth edition
1 3 5 7 9 10 8 6 4 2

This almanac is published by Abbeville Press, www.abbeville.com.
For bulk and premium sales, call 1-800-ARTBOOK.
Customized covers and complimentary point-of-sale displays are available with bulk orders of the almanac.